GUGGENHEIM
INTERNATIONAL AWARD
1964

THE SOLOMON R. GUGGENHEIM MUSEUM, NEW YORK

Published by The Solomon R. Guggenheim Foundation, New York, 1963   All Rights Reserved   Library of Congress Card Catalog Number: 63-14482

Printed in The Netherlands

PARTICIPATING INSTITUTIONS

HONOLULU ACADEMY OF ARTS

AKADEMIE DER KÜNSTE, BERLIN

THE NATIONAL GALLERY OF CANADA, OTTAWA

MUSEO NACIONAL DE BELLAS ARTES, BUENOS AIRES

JOHN AND MABLE RINGLING MUSEUM OF ART, SARASOTA

The Guggenheim International Award was established by the Trustees of The Solomon R. Guggenheim Foundation in 1956. The objective was then, and is now, to create major contemporary art awards carrying with them preeminent national and international prestige. The hope of the Foundation has been that the Award will not only be significant in the field of art but will also be an important manifestation of international good will.

The awards and the accompanying exhibitions in 1956, 1958 and 1960 were presented with the cooperation of the International Council of Museums, the International Association of Art Critics, and the International Association of Plastic Arts. The 1964 Award has been administered by the Guggenheim Museum and has become the responsibility of the Director and his staff. The Museum's Curator has travelled to more than thirty countries and has, while selecting works for the exhibition, sought guidance from individual members of the three international organizations and, in addition, consulted many other sources. The Jury of Award consists of Hans Hofmann, a senior painter of world-wide reputation, Arnold Rüdlinger, a distinguished museum director, and Werner Haftmann, well known historian of modern art.

On behalf of the Trustees of The Solomon R. Guggenheim Foundation I would like to express our gratitude to those individuals and organizations which have so generously contributed to the achievement of the Fourth Guggenheim International Award.

Harry F. Guggenheim, President

This exhibition was chosen during an intensive one-year's search that led the Guggenheim Museum's Curator, Mr. Lawrence Alloway, through the United States, Canada, Latin America, Europe and the Orient.

The following considerations have determined the selection:

Not more than one hundred paintings were to be assembled to safeguard their relaxed and spacious presentation and to prevent an oversaturation from which giant shows often suffer. Not more than five works were to be chosen from any one country to assure the broadly international character of the event. All works, to be eligible, had to be executed during the last three years—a rule made to stress the current validity of the selection.

As a matter of institutional policy there is a commitment toward inclusiveness in matters stylistic. As in all areas involving selective judgment at the Guggenheim Museum, idiomatic allegiances are considered to be irrelevant to the central problem of quality. The selection for the Guggenheim International Award exhibition, therefore, is not concerned with the presence or absence, the numerical strength or weakness, of any particular idiom.

The need for a unified and compatible exhibition concept does arise and presents the organizing museum with certain choices: It would have been possible, for example, to select an exhibition made up of the old masters of the modern movement. A totally different approach would have been required had it been the intention to bring to the fore young and unknown painters of talent and accomplishment. Instead of these alternatives, the exhibitions follows a central course. It is primarily concerned with the generation born in the first two decades of our century —painters who now have reached maturity and whose life work stands before us in its fullness. Their work is known although international recognition or fame may not always attach itself to it. They are, in the characteristic instance, leaders of a working generation, rather than a myth on the one hand or a mere promise on the other. This rule is not without its exceptions; however, whenever an active, current, leadership could support the full burden of a nation's art, both the old master and the young talent categories remained marginal.

Although mentioned in the last place, the very first consideration has always been the excellence of specific paintings. As in the case with the awards themselves, the selection too, must be seen as an endorsement of a particular work rather than a vote of confidence in a painter's general attainments.

One or two artists who would have merited inclusion were not invited because of their stated unwillingness to be shown in this or in any group show. The wish to be omitted from eligibility in the Award has also been honored in a few instances and the names of painters participating under this restricted condition are marked in the catalogue list.

Finally, it must be taken for granted that no one charged with a global task of the dimensions of the Fourth Guggenheim International Award exhibition would want to deny the role played by the opportunity of specific confrontations with works of art, or the lack of it. Nor would one wish to exaggerate the objectivity of the selecting process or argue against the existence of a legitimate bias. It is, on the contrary, through the elimination of all mechanical procedures and through the application of an individual intelligence that such a choice as this assumes its ultimate validity.

Thomas M. Messer, Director

ACKNOWLEDGMENTS

I am most grateful to the following for their assistance in the preparation of this exhibition and catalogue: Joachim Jean Aberbach, New York, Topazia Alliata, Rome, Troels Andersen, Copenhagen, Peter Anker, Oslo, Miguel Arroyo, Caracas, Guy Atkins, London, Arnold Belkin, Mexico City, Thomas Birch, Copenhagen, Mr. and Mrs. Alfredo Bonino, Buenos Aires, Denise Breteau, Paris, Peter Cochrane, London, Daniel Cordier, Paris, Samuel Dubiner, Tel Aviv, Arne Ekstrom, New York, George Elliott, Chile, H. R. Fischer, London, Karl Flinker, Paris, Jean Fournier, Paris, Suzi Gablik, New York, Winfred Gaul, Dusseldorf, Tatsuhiko Heima, New York, Thomas B. Hess, New York, K. G. Hultèn, Stockholm, Francisco Icaza, Mexico City, Thomas Ichinose, Tokyo, Paul Jenkins, Paris, Emilio del Junco, Toronto, Barry Kernerman, Tel Aviv, Max Kozloff, New York, John Lefebre, New York, Albert Loeb, New York, Beatrice Monti, Milan, Robert Murray, New York, Beatrice Perry, New York, Zora Sweet Pinney, Los Angeles, Denise René, Paris, Per Rom, Oslo, Dr. Werner Schmalenbach, Dusseldorf, Pierre Schneider, Paris, Arturo Schwartz, Milan, Shinichi Segui, Tokyo, Kusuo Shimizu, Tokyo, José Gomez Sicre, Washington, D.C., Peter Stroud, Bennington, Vermont, Yoshiaki Tono, Tokyo, Harry Torczyner, New York, Edith Zerlaut-Rauscher, Paris.

My thanks are due also to Lucy Lippard for her indispensable work on the documentation in the catalogue. For translations of documentary material, I wish to thank Lillemor Engberg for her work on the Danish texts; Simona Morini for the German and French sections; and M. Tinga for the Dutch.

For their extensive contributions to the catalogue, gratitude is due the following members of the Museum Staff: Carol Fuerstein, who edited the catalogue, and, with Maurice Tuchman, compiled the biographies and bibliographies (in addition, Mr. Tuchman kindly read through the manuscript for me); Barbara Burn and Linda Konheim, who assisted them in preparing material and seeing the book through the press; Alice Hildreth, who worked closely with me on every phase of the exhibition and the catalogue.

L. A.

LENDERS TO THE EXHIBITION

Julian J. and Joachim Jean Aberbach, New York
Miss Isabeile Collin-DuFresne, New York
Jean Fournier, Paris
Mr. and Mrs. Arnold Ginsburg, New York
Sonja Henie and Niels Onstad, Los Angeles
Joseph H. Hirshhorn Collection, New York
Tomás Marentes, Mexico City
Beatrice and Hart Perry, New York
Jon Nicholas Streep, New York

Museo de Bellas Artes, Caracas

Galleria dell'Ariete, Milan
Galeria Bonino, Buenos Aires and New York
Galerie Breteau, Paris
Galerie Daniel Cordier, Paris
Galerie d'Eendt, Amsterdam
Galerie Karl Flinker, Paris
The Hanover Gallery, London
Alexander Iolas Gallery, New York
The Isaacs Gallery, Toronto
Galerie Israel, Tel Aviv
Martha Jackson Gallery, New York
Galerie K.-K., Copenhagen
M. Knoedler & Co., New York and Paris
Samuel M. Kootz Gallery Inc., New York
Lefebre Gallery, New York
Marlborough, London and New York
Pierre Matisse Gallery, New York
Minami Gallery, Tokyo
Jerrold Morris Gallery, Toronto
Galleria d'Arte del Naviglio, Milan
Galerie Denise René, Paris
Galerie Alfred Schmela, Dusseldorf
Galerie Stadler, Paris
The Zora Gallery, Los Angeles

INTRODUCTION

> *One has not the alternative of speaking of London as a whole, for*
> *the simple reason that there is no such thing as the whole of it . . .*
> *Rather it is a collection of many wholes, and of which of them*
> *is it most important to speak?*

Henry James. *Essays in London and Elsewhere*, New York, 1893, p. 27.

This exhibition is not a chronicle, because a chronicle sets events into successive order. The purpose of this exhibition is to sample paintings of the last three years, a period that is treated here as a single unit of time. It is not historical sequence that is the point of the exhibition, but a statement about current possibilities. Essentially I envisage this collection of paintings as a dialogue. All the contributors to the dialogue are painters, and this is the show's unity; on the other hand, the painters represent divergent possibilities within the continuum of art, as it is at present conceivable and practiced. A dialogue is "a conversation between two or more persons" or "a literary work in the form of a conversation between two or more persons" (Oxford Universal Dictionary). It is not, therefore, a form in which one expects a speedy conclusion of discussion, or the emergence of sudden champions. On the contrary, it is a flexible and continuing form which involves the artist with his contemporaries, but not with them only. The past of art is implicit in the dialogue, not simply as a store of models, but as a potentially active and present participant. The work of living painters continually modifies retroactively the meanings available in the art of the past. In this sense, the present exhibition is not only a sample of topical works, though it is that, it is, also, part of a relationship one has today with the whole of art, as it is implicated in the paintings actually here.

Ortega has pointed out that "it is not only those born in the same year who are the same age in life and history, but those who are born within a zone of dates".[1] Thus, although the present exhibition samples the paintings of only three years, any short period is capacious, in that various generations are at work within it. There are various theories of the effective length of a generation, from the 15 years for which Ortega opts, to the 30 years more usually maintained. The shorter period seems closer to the rate of change in painting since the 1870's. The generations are not clearly stratified, one above another. On the contrary, there are affiliations and antagonisms working across the age-groups as well as within them. Such conditions must prepare us for an unhomogeneous range of styles, for diversity as a global fact.

A dialogue exemplifies variety rather than hierarchy. As an example, consider the different American artists in this exhibition. Hans Hofmann is a painter who regards the area of the painting as a place within which discrete formal elements strenuously compete until they arrive at equilibrium. This is true even of his softest and quickest paintings. Barnett Newman, on the other hand, treats the surface of his painting wholistically, and animates it in one, with a single flood or band of color, without internal diversification. Philip Guston works the surface with an intense anxiety until the piled-up marks of the brush hesitantly reach a luxurious fullness; his is an inhabited space, but not one decodable into a clearly-described world. Comments of this kind about painting may appear to be about technical and formal matters; in fact, this is not a restriction in human value. Characteristic of art in the 20th century is the increasing intervention of the technical and formal means in the meaning of a work of art. (This is as true of figurative as it is of abstract painting; it is as true of art historians as it is of current reviewers.) The formality of a painting has too often been treated separately from the meaning, as a property peeled off from the human content. There has been no lack of formal analysis in the 20th century; only a lack of feeling for its expressive capacity. Robert Motherwell's *Elegies for the Spanish Republic*, the 70th of which is shown here, raise problems about how they can, in fact, signify "Spain" (see *Anthology*). To discuss them, merely, as black flat patterns is inadequate. Adolph Gottlieb's *Roman Three* presents a central green disc with a bright yellow aureole and three patches of color (brown, yellow, green) on a darker yellow field; these color areas, in relation to the background, involve one in signs of a grouping and relationship that relate to the ways one orders all experiences. The ordering activity of the artist is an analogue of our own learning and sorting out of experiences.

Basic, of course, to the image of dialogue is another idea: that of diversity. There are certain difficulties about maintaining diversity as an ideal because, traditionally, art and artists have been subjected to very strong hierarchic ordering. Artists themselves, since the 15th century, have been much preoccupied with what is "fine" and what is "high" in their art, and this has continually involved the promotion of one genre or one style above another. Historically-minded writers and painters have imposed similar priorities, by tracing a main line from, say, Greece to Rome to Paris, as in French Classicism of the 17th century. Such habits of ordering persist today: for example, a remarkable quantity of theory about abstract art has depended on an assumption of the historical necessity of the route from late 19th century realism to 20th century abstraction. The idea of the dialogue, however, is an alternative to such linear or hierarchic reductions of experience. Then, art can be regarded as an area of the greatest freedom, in which plural choices co-exist. Art is not like science in the sense that it possesses a constantly growing body of knowledge;

it is more like a field of increasing reach and complexity. Connectivity and insights are linked in this ample network. If, in this exhibition, variety is maintained as a standard, it is not because one is afraid to make judgements, or hesitates to set a value. On the contrary, it is because only a recognition of complexity is adequate to a complex situation. As the number of artists has grown, and as the audience for art has grown, the conditions for really divergent forms of expression have appeared, far beyond, say, Florence in the 15th century, which was already significantly stratified. The shift from an aesthetic of shortage to one of abundance can be exemplified in many other fields. For example, Alfred P. Sloan, Jr. in his memoirs of the early days of the automobile industry observes that Henry Ford's "basic conception of one car in one utility model at an even lower price was what the world mainly needed at the time . . . Yet Mr. [William C.] Durant's feeling for variety in automobiles, however undefined it was then, came closer to the trend of the industry as it evolved in later years. Today each major producer makes a variety of car".[2]

Dialogue, as a way of defining art, has advantages over the Model-T type of art criticism. Not only does it accord with our impulses at a level of generosity and curiosity, rather than at a level of restriction and exclusion, it is closer to the real abundance of modern art. The consumption of art (its display and criticism, as well as its purchase) has changed radically, at least as much as, and possibly more than, its production. There is greater continuity between the artists of the 20th century and certain artists of the past, engrossed in operational and conceptual aspects of the art of painting, than exists between the spectator of art today and past consumers. The instant availability of world art and new art is one factor that decisively separates us from the past. This emerged as a problem in the 19th century (when revival styles were a sign of the awareness of stylistic diversity), but has developed to its maximum point only at mid-century. Another change, which involves the spectator as well as the artist, is the difficult topic of the relation between national styles and international art.

Nationality is no easier to define in connection with art than with any other field, though it requires at least a shared language, a shared territory, and some common ideals and memories. From the standpoint of national identity, however we define it, the present international style of abstract art is often criticized for sacrificing local traditions to rootless efficacity. As the traveler and the magazine reader both know there is a great deal of provincial criticism of international art at present. The fact that art, like other human activities, proceeds from, and builds on the current "state of knowledge" in the field cannot be suppressed or evaded, however. In the 20th century there is an unrivalled knowledge available to the artist of the art of the past and of the rest of the world in addition, an artist's own work is liable to be distributed, both in reproduction and in the original, far beyond his personal reach. International art styles have existed before and, indeed, art naturally spreads along all available channels of distribution. The Gothic, the Baroque, Romanticism, were all international in their reach and central in their cultural value. What is new is the speed with which information is transmitted and the fullness of the message, the one-to-one correspondence of the original work and its surrogates. One reason for the suspicion of international style, as it is linked with modern communication techniques, is a fear that the autonomy of the work of art may be vitiated by over-use.

Essential to any defense of international art is a definition of art which relates it to the expanded and accelerating communications network to which we are all plugged in. Fashion and war, the mass media and high art, are distributed globally and, though subject to local modification, do not rest securely in local areas. The diffusion of the work of art, by means of museums and galleries, books and magazines, into the world of mass communications raises problems. The reality of art for an artist has to do with an experience felt within the creative act. By comparison, the distribution of the works beyond his own precinct, *arrondisement*, postal area, canton, or island can only be another kind of experience, and a comparatively impersonal one. The work of art, which he knows from the inside, has entered a collective and anonymous life. It is anonymous in the sense that its uniqueness may be reduced by comparison with other artists and their works. In an exhibition like the present, for instance, paintings are placed in relations that may mean something to me but may be irrelevant to the intentions or values of the artists. By putting together works from different parts of the world, general ideas, possible constants, emerge in ways that may seem to threaten to reduce the concrete original work to the status of a diagram or an example.

The problem which must be faced, to resolve one's doubts about the role of the original work of art in a world of so many entertaining exhibitions and books, is this: has the work of art one meaning, and one only? To answer "yes" to this question is either to commit oneself to a highly idealistic notion of art or to ignore all our knowledge, introspective and sociological, of the range of human responses. It seems that everything conspires to make the meaning of art problematic. Psychoanalysis has posited meanings unknown to the artist in the work and iconography has demonstrated meanings in art that have been forgotten and unavailable to generations of spectators. Abstract art, once secured in a Platonic realm of essences, has lost its purity and can now be considered as iconography. However it is an iconography without explicit literary sources; it is the repetition and modification by the artist of his characteristic image which yields the iconographic meaning. The work of art is especially subject to variable readings, not only because acts of perception and interpretation are fantastically and humanly diverse, but because our form-perception is only approximately served by the verbal order we confer on most of the world.

In addition, the mobility of the work of art today makes us especially aware of the role of context in interpreting art. In the studio, which is the best place to see paintings, the spectator is as close as he is likely to get to the work of the artist both literally and imaginatively. In a one-man exhibition at a gallery, the painter *may* be able to present a cogently related group of works, which feed each other, like, say, a poet's arrangement of his own poems. The Jeanne Duval poems of Baudelaire (xx-xxxv in the first edition of *Les Fleurs du Mal*) have an internal coherence created by cross-references and recurring images. This cluster-effect, when realized by paintings in a gallery, can create an extraordinary environmental sense, in which the works fully become the spectator's world (See *Anthology:* Turnbull). Mixed exhibitions offer another resource of meaning: connections and relationships occur, between one painting and another, one country and another. One witnesses the sudden or covert, willing or reluctant, convergence of separated human beings, the emergence of points of unity and constancy. In the case of the present exhibition, it may be possible to demonstrate style as an international fact, as what is constant and shared by works of art produced in widely separated places at the same time. At present, the concept of "style" tends to be identified by artists with mannerism and cliché; in fact, it is simply a way of discussing one of the relationships (i.e. formal resemblance) that exists among works of art.

All ways of presenting works of art, all ways of writing about them, and all the ways of reproducing them, have inherent limitations. Writers who are infatuated or preoccupied with one episode in the sequence of meanings that a work of art carries oppose the alternate meanings which arise from, say, mobility or distribution. Objections to reproductions are usually of this sort and so are complaints about the excess of exhibitions to be seen around the world. In the past, works of art have traditionally been associated, for long periods, with particular locations, a city, a palace, a chapel, a wall. This intimately time-binding aspect of art endures today but now co-exists with an alternative approach which depends on the mobility of works of art. The processes of printed communication have made, in André Malraux's phrase, an imaginary museum in which meanings are found in isolation from the work of art's original functions. It is a powerful extension of the kind of handy museum which prints have made possible to their owners since the 16th century. As museums have developed away from exclusive duties of conservation, another form of display has appeared which combines the Faustian freedom of each imaginary museum's curator with the physical presence of original works of art. (In this respect museums have developed out of the 18th century salon which exposed large collections of modern works by assorted artists.) A museum exhibition, therefore, is somewhere between the symbolism of reproductions and the authenticity, as it were, of the originals in a hallowed site. Viewed in this way, mixed exhibitions may offer lines of argument, in which the paintings act as examples of something or other, but, at the same time, far more than in a book or a magazine, the works are present, embodying, in their own scale and facture, the decisions of their makers.

Belief that the work of art has variable meanings does not mean that anything goes, that paintings are simply stimuli to provoke wild, optional responses.

Abstract paintings are unlike Rorschach Tests and figurative paintings are unlike Thematic Apperception Tests. On the other hand, paintings are exceptionally complex structures and, hence, variety of interpretation is liable to be part of the historical meaning of works of art. The different responses of different people, or one's own changing responses, have a limited validity; each meaning has its particular appropriateness or, if it has not, it is not likely to be remembered or effective. A painting, experienced in isolation, or as part of a group by one artist, or as one of a crowd in a survey exhibition, retains certain stable factors, that are neither stretched nor worn down by repeated use. Leonardo's *Mona Lisa* has been the subject of every kind of contextualising, including a renewal of publicity when the painting was loaned to the United States recently. One popular response to the popularity of the painting was to reject it as having become a cliché. My own feeling was that it was still, or, perhaps, again, meaningful as a painting, but that, by comparison *L.H.O.O.Q.*, Marcel Duchamp's grafiti on a reproduction of the *Mona Lisa*, was now boring. What preserves painting is its concreteness, its internal solidity, its self-composure, its presence as an ordered structure.

There is, obviously, an international style in post-war art. Sometimes one country may be the origin of a particular way of painting; sometimes the shared qualities emerge spontaneously. An international style does not, of course, impose uniformity on its members. In fact, many of the artists themselves recoil from the notion of a globally unified style and prefer to emphasize national or regional characteristics. American painters, for example, are more interested in the ways they may be American than in the way they are international. Josef Mikl said in conversation that it was not post-war gestural art that he felt an affinity with, but, as a Viennese, the Danube School. He compared his brush work to 16th century landscape paintings from the Danube Valley. What he meant can be seen by a quotation from a Viennese art historian. Otto Benesch describes Altdorfer as painting not the isolated beauty of separate forms but "the total impression, the exuberance and growth of nature itself". "In Altdorfer's painting, the objects seem to be colored condensations of atmosphere" and his "handling of the brush like a drawing pen contributes to this unification".[3] It is a fact that regional identifications of this kind persist throughout this international period.

This identification works for the artist in 20th century Vienna and, once pointed out, it can be recognized, though not, perhaps, spontaneously discovered. There is a difference between this sophisticated and covert, though deeply-felt, relation to a national tradition and earlier regional artists. The first school of Latham St. Martin, for instance, was ostentatiously regional in a way that Mikl is not, and would not want to be. The fact that his art is both international and national leads to a changed experience of local traditions. Artists who make their own personal sense of location into relevant and usable traditions, in a period of copious international contacts, are certainly not cultural primitivists. Perhaps we can talk of the *re*-nationalization of artists who revive, knowingly, their background; it is done without abandoning their internationalism but, equally, without becoming parochial. "What I learnt in Paris is *leaving me*, and . . . I am returning to the ideas I had in the country before I knew the impressionists",[4] Van Gogh wrote. Van Gogh was "re-becoming Dutch", as Émile Bernard pointed out, but Holland was not the same as it had been at Zundert where he was born.

In this exhibition, national characteristics can often be detected, but they are always, I think, the result of re-nationalization. It is, that is to say, the choice of artists resuming a tradition with which they feel intimate, with which they feel "at home". The national characteristics are not an expression of the *genius loci* in their bones, a blind national genius spontaneously erupting to destroy the superficial continuities of international style. The position of painters in Spain, for example, seems typical of this changed situation. They have adopted, knowingly and lucidly, a certain image of national style which they have nurtured and sponsored. For their artistic purposes they have used a romantic image of Spain as parched, dark, tragic. This has been taken literally by many writers but it is, in fact, a formal and constructed image, at the service of a way of painting. A key figure in Spanish re-nationalism is, of course, Goya, who is, also continually invoked by South American artists who feel strongly the need for Hispano-American links. The real counterpart to re-nationalized images of Vienna or Spain is not the country as it is experienced by its least mobile and alert natives. Rather it must be recognized as a constructed image, like, say, the imagined Ireland of W. B. Yeats' *The Celtic Twilight*.

The *Cobra* group, formed in 1948, united artists from Denmark, Belgium, and Holland as a *North*-European style consciously opposed to French rationalism and Mediterranean poise. Corneille records the rapport he felt on a journey to Denmark, soon after World War II, with two other Dutch artists, Karel Appel and Constant. They met Carl-Henning Pedersen and Ejler Bille in Copenhagen and "the very same day we got acquainted with the works of the Danes which we knew only from reproduction. In a vast hall, opposite the Osterport-station, our friends' paintings were hanging. Life knows emotions which remain with one forever, and the first look at these paintings gave us such a sensation . . . We found in Denmark people who had fought for years against any formalism".[5] The *Cobra* artists, taking their lead from the Danes, combined painterly improvisation with the development of a spectacular iconography of men and beasts.

Asger Jorn criticized André Breton's definition of surrealism as "pure psychic automatism" because, he argued "It is impossible to express oneself in a purely psychic way. The very act of expressing oneself is a physical act which materializes the idea. Psychic automatism is, therefore, organically bound to physical automatism".[6] He wrote this in 1948, and he expresses what was a widely shared dissatisfaction with surrealism at this time. Surrealist ideas were influential and current but their realization in works of art tended to appear as dry and crabbed. Surrealist automatism, for instance, was usually graphic and small in scale. Jorn demands a frankly and fully physical embodiment of automatic techniques. This is certainly parallel to, though geographically separate from, what was happening in the United States where Gorky and Pollock, among others, also combined automatism with painterly rather than graphic scale and procedures. In addition, Cobra imagery sometimes resembles Pollock's early work in which magical and sexual human figures emerge out of a swarm of ripely painted cubist forms. It is significant that Pollock, though he developed a pure abstract style out of his myth-laden figurative works, returned, easily and fluently in 1951, to a figurative mode. *Cobra* artists, on the other hand, have been consistently figurative. The point is that a common problem was, in the 40s, faced independently and solved differently, though with points of similarity.

One *Cobra* painter, Egill Jacobsen, writing about another, Pedersen, states: "In Denmark, the artistic language of folk and fairy tales is used in so-called abstract art, based on our centuries-old experience".[7] This basis in folk-art is an assertion of what is common, more or less, to everybody. Thus, an art of re-nationalization here employs materials which, though rooted in Danish lore, have an affinity with other countries, also. (Folklore, like the unconscious mind, is presumed to be ubiquitous.) The painters, Ernesto Deira, Jorge de la Vega, Rómulo Macció, and Luis Felipe Noé, as well as Jacobo Borges, benefit to some extent from *Cobra's* influence, but their style is perfectly viable with their native South American culture. Thus, re-nationalism is flexible rather than constraining, adaptive rather than nostalgic.

Given the amount of art now being produced, and given the fact that not every potential of art is simultaneously available all the time, there are bound to be regularities in world art. One of the ways of describing these constants is in terms of art movements or, if that seems too formal and compact a term, tendencies. The dialogue is between artists, but it is, also, between larger groups; between generations, or between alternate traditions, or between various tendencies which display different qualities and which imply different ideas. The existence of shared themes, of stylistic correspondences or common assumptions, means, simply, that the dialogue has super-personal, as well as personal, aspects. Without lessening the individuality of the artists concerned, it is possible to point out, within the work of eighty-two painters, various points of contact. The constellations that I hope to indicate are not the only ones; they are not necessarily the final ones to be made. The fact that order is always a provisional and arbitrary act, however, is not a sufficient reason for not attempting it.

Speed of gesture, brevity in time, characterize one trend of recent painting. Rapidly-made works, are, in one way, the culmination of the autographic definition of art that emerged in the Renaissance. As H. W. Janson has pointed out: "works of art were coming to be valued as embodiments of the artist's individual style; and since this style was as personal as a signature, it could be seen only in works that were autographic, i.e. originals. The new attitude gradually gave rise to a special appreciation of tentative, unfinished, and fragmentary works such as drawings and sketches executed in a direct and spontaneous way".[8] In the open texture of much recent painting, the graphic mark is intimately revelatory of the artist. The size of these paintings, often around the scale of a man, encourages one to identify with the human reach of the gestures tangibly recorded, as tracks, on the face of the canvas. Somebody estimated, once, that de Kooning's line travelled at 94½ miles per hour. By working fast it is possible, for a time, to elude the customs of slower work, to astonish oneself: an unexpected contour lassoes an unhackneyed image. Pollock worked quickly to cover the whole surface of his drip paintings so that his concluding decisions were arrived at not as the result of pre-planning but as a response to the developing form of the painting. The work of art, as a result, is narrowed to a point in time defined by spontaneity and self-correcting disciplines. K. R. H. Sonderborg's work notes give the times of his drawings (3.8.60:21h 09 to 21h21), with the precision and minuteness of a sports writer or a television commercial. If you see a row of television commercials, one after another, the profiles of slower, more classical, forms obstinately appear within these apparently ejaculatory messages. In a seven second commercial, the end can be signalled too fast; in a fifteen second commercial, the story line can falter and drag. The point is, a great acuity is demanded in the fast forms of expression; slower values are compressed, but not abandoned. De Kooning once compared this way of working, which characterizes his later paintings, to throwing dice, rather than to playing poker.[9]

Matter painting, as I would call the use of dense heavy pigments, weighted with sand or marble dust, laid over plastic or plaster grounds, translates space into weight. Spatial definition in such paintings is achieved by a sculpturesque use of mass, as the body literally present. It is, perhaps, the opposite of gestural painting, in which the body swings athletically free, or appears to. In the heavy pastes, laid down and dragged around, color counts for less than tactility; immediacy means less than the evocation of time. In a painting like that of Antoni Tàpies', the ancient wall suggests dilapidation but, in its delicacy, the artist implies affection towards the surviving artifacts of man. In a painting like Bram Bogart's, a dense primal image of landscape is created, unchanged, as it were, since the beginning of time. In terms of figurative art, the use of massive impasto can be linked, as in the paintings of Evert Lundquist and Graham Coughtry, with forms described less according to visual appearance than to a tactile sense of mass. Bulky and resistant bodies, crowded and sloping spaces, are realized by the weight of the paint, heaped and pressed, in analogues of our bodily sense of weight, balance, and touch.

What might be called Field Painting is represented in this exhibition by paintings from Spain, America, England. Here large planes of colors spread across the canvas so that the spectator is deluged or surrounded by the sensation of a single, or main, color. There is a tendency in other forms of painting to use, or at least to imply, the presence of all colors in the painting. A big Léger, for example, always contains red and blue and green; a big Picasso, even if greyed, implies the existence of a pulverized spectrum of full color. Field painting, on the other hand, minimizes or expunges color contrast; all the colors come from one part of the spectrum;

the effect is of irradiation and expansion of color, rather than of internal modification and complexity. Miró's large expanse of blue picks up a theme of his work in the 20s, the empty "skies" which were crossed by a meandering line or inhabited by a single floating object. Newman's *The Third* has a solid shining intensity of orange, which is entirely different from the wavering and nuanced screen of Turnbull's yellow painting *Mango*. Paintings of this kind demonstrate anew that nothing is more subtle, nothing more complex, than simplicity. There is no question of these paintings being intended as objects, free of the sensuality of painting techniques and free of the illusions of space. The perception of such large areas, especially when viewed close up, confronts the spectator with an environmental expression. The color field is large enough and strong enough to provoke after-images, so that each spectator introduces his own subjective modifications of the great color plane. The color area itself is never smoothed or neatened, as it is in rigorous geometric art; field painting, on the contrary, retains, in its traces of process, the hand of the artist, as much as its total form embodies his concept.

Monochrome painting, in Europe or Asia, has links with Field Painting, in its condensation of all colors into one, or a very few. However, where Field Painting is associated with a very direct and restrained method of painting, sensuous but reticent, monochrome painting covers a wider range. At one point it touches, in the shaped canvases of Lucio Fontana, on the creation of picture-objects, and in Enrico Castellani one sees an interest in regularity of structure that approaches aspects of geometric art. At another point, in Tomoyasu Murakami, for instance, it becomes a primal substance from which anything might grow or climb; in Arnulf Rainer the moist plane of color is, perhaps, the floor of a Danube forest. The discovery of the structural and expressive possibilities of monochrome might be compared to our increasing knowledge of outer space. Where once there was a vacuum there is now a plasma which supports electromagnetic radiation and magnetic fields; outer space has, as it were, a climate, and weather. Single colors, once regarded as empty in isolation, now reveal a physiognomy and activity. The outer space imagery is not intended to suggest an analogy between art and space exploration, only to suggest the way in which our knowledge is continually extended into areas regarded as blank, fruitless, or deserted.

Several factors have combined to perplex the once apparently settled area of geometric abstract art. On one hand, the definition of geometry has widened, so that geometrical terms are equally applicable to continuous free forms and to distinct Euclidean ones. Both the mystical and pseudo-technological rationales, of Kandinsky and Malevich respectively, are totally inadequate to the mid-century artist who makes a searching use of geometric forms. A possible term for this area might be the rigorous tradition, for it is consistently characterized by a sparing and systematic use of a limited number of formal elements. Increasingly, this art has depended on the methodical development of forms or their repetition.[10] This is often seen as an additive structure of identical repeating units, in which the single bit and the whole configuration make a continuous process. Vasarely, for example, though he often bunches forms in large and small areas, begins his paintings with a kind of binary system. This on/off, black/white system persists in his paintings, however much he subsequently diversifies the forms. Combined with the rigorous use of limited forms, the study of perception has brought the creation of unstable or ambiguous forms, paradoxically, to a high point of control and precision. "Precision", as Vasarely said to me, "is subjective."

With the failure of the theory, usual in the early 20th century, that geometry was the equivalent of absolute and essential forms, geometric form is now recognized as ambiguous, engaging, and useful though not, as it were, sacred. Now it is particularly linked with high development of color, far beyond early modern art in its control and its vivacity. In Max Bill and Richard P. Lohse mathematical organizations are used to invent and control subtle configurations in which color shines, clear, hard and intricate; Peter Stroud overlays his symmetrical format with what he calls an "anti-structure" of elusive color. Baertling relates his art to a traditional, early 20th century Utopia, but in practice he, too, uses the sophisticated structural play of the rational development of geometric abstract art. Black in his painting acts both as a contour and as a plane, so that it is sometimes outline and sometimes a color.

Man, in paintings of the *Cobra* group, exists at a level below that of, say, urban man in the 20th century. As Jorn discusses man [see *Anthology*] he is not defined by identity cards and dog tags or by shades of individuality. Man is treated at a biological and survival level, with occasional elevation to Kings in Pedersen and frequent excursions into animal contact and metamorphosis in all the *Cobra* artists. Henri Michaux wrote: "There is an inner phantom that one should be able to paint, instead of painting the nose, the eyes, and the hair that are outside" and "I would like to be able to draw the effluvia that flow from one person to another".[11] These statements are close to *Cobra* iconography. Regarding the separate artists as a group we can distinguish the following typical situations. (1) The single figure, often a head, partly subcutaneous, a projection of the self of the painter, and partly legendary and apparitional: (2) The couple, in sexual contact, or combat; frequently this pairing is a kind of encounter, as of Death and Life, or animal and human. The encounter of human and animal occurs in expressionist forerunners of *Cobra*, such as Nolde and Munch.[12] Its origin may be in Gauguin's *La Perte du Pucelage*, with its encounter of nude girl and fox. (3) The crowd, the horde, the swarm, which can be an Ensor-like carnival rabble, or a Dante-esque river of sinners, or a tree packed with heads. The flow of the image makes the paint act like an ectoplasm out of which human forms condense. In all these images, of the one, the couple, and the many, painterly improvisation picks up themes of Expressionism and fantastic art and makes of their iconography a natural confessional stream.

An aspect of recent painting, which has not been sufficiently recognized in general terms, is the iconographical explosion (of which Pop Art is a part). In the present exhibition iconographical complexity is marked, certainly, in Paul Delvaux, René Magritte, Matta, Öyvind Fahlström, and R. B. Kitaj. Delvaux extends the city and dream imagery of di Chirico, so that urban, nocturnal, and sexual themes mingle. Magritte presents puzzles about objects which echo to confuse both something called life and something called art (*see Anthology*). His iconography is devoted to paradoxes of communication and description: "is it Granada I see or Asbury Park?" Matta once responded to the suggestion that his imagery was reminiscent of science fiction by rejecting the link: "either Science Fiction is Science Fiction, or I am", he declared. Nevertheless his imagery has always been full of quotes and allusions, stretched or impacted, to many sources: technology, comics, public occasions such as trials, games, and so on. Fahlstrom, with his *Dr. Livingstone, I Presume*, makes a scrambled version of all the (non-color) comic books one has seen. The techniques of naturalistic representation are there, but all deprived, or partially severed from, their original referents. Kitaj brings into his painting allusions to various literary sources and to various periods and places of recent history. His subject is connections and cross-references between the figures and occasions of his imagery, as well as scrutiny of the conventional nature of representation itself. Dubuffet has shown scholarship as well as dramatic power as an image-maker; the iconography of the city, the desert, and the garden, which recurs in his work, has a power of tapping the resonance of existing traditions, while being solidly and personally eloquent. The flattened automobiles which drivers inhabit in the Paris streets, for instance, are like wrecked automobiles and trees, flattened anatomies and lily-ponds. Each specific subject in Dubuffet has a way of opening out into the rest of his art.

Giacometti and Francis Bacon are both represented by standing nudes, close to the spectator in the foreground of the picture space. In both there are references to traditional iconography (particularly in the Bacon) and in both the paint itself is conspicuous (particularly in the Giacometti). The point to be made is that the figurative paintings in this exhibition reveal, as much as is the case in the abstract paintings, the intervention of formal and technical means into the image. Balthus' painting, for instance, has summary flattenings and erasures, in which the body of the painting is asserted through the screen of the descriptive image. This is one of several points at which connections exist between abstract and figurative painting. Abstract art, originally, needed to be separated, as fully as possible, from figurative art. Now, however, with the presence of human meaning in abstract art stressed anew and with the formal and, so to say, artificial elements of figurative art recognized more strongly, connections between the so-called poles can now be seen. (The all-over composition, so often noted in abstract art, occurs also in figurative painters, like Jorn and Alechinsky.) With the increasing recognition of the complexity of figurative art, which has so often been discussed merely as the poor half of a pair with abstract art, it may be that an adequate esthetic of figurative art and its problems may emerge. Most of the criticism of such painting has been unambitious and desultory.

There has been a general shift in our attitude to art, since World War II, and one of the ways in which it can be traced is in a new emphasis in our way of speaking and writing about art. Typical of the new usage is a phrase of Malraux's about Fautrier's *Otages*, coined in 1945: he called them "ideograms of suffering". Writing and sign-systems have been invoked before in connection with art (Symbolists and Surrealists used it a good deal), but in the last twenty years it has increased significantly. The acceptance of the idea of art as signs has important consequences. Instead of art being isolated, in a timeless terminal state, it is insistently linked, with our life, or with the artist's, or with the humanity common to the artist and the spectator. The sharpened and sophisticated eye for formal values, learned early in the century, is, of course, neither abandoned nor relaxed. It is simply that the humanity of the decisions embodied in the work is stressed with a new passion and conviction. Numerous exhibitions and articles, in line with this cultural shift, have been devoted to the significative aspects of art. The importance of the renewed interest in art as signs is not bound to its gestural and graphic aspects (this is, in reality, simply one part of the picture) but involves our whole conception of art as human evidence.

A persistent theme of modern art criticism has been the decline, eclipse, and disappearance of easel painting. It has been buried repeatedly, by idealists with an operatic dream of synthesis, by educators with a standard of utility to which art must conform, and by political critics demanding a legible public art. The large size of post-war paintings and the display of forms in all-over configurations have also been nominated as beyond easel painting.[13] In fact, viewed historically, large canvases are not unusual since the 16th century and easel painting has always been particularly the medium in which experiment is possible and in which various modes of organization have co-existed. This is not to accommodate new all-over painting to past models but to suggest, rather, that it is within the technical limits of easel painting as historically defined. In addition, the resources of painting have been juggled with and blurred by mixed media artists who combine literal objects and painted space. In this exhibition, however, the homogeneity of the painted surface, with a minimum of collage elements, has been stressed. The fact that an exhibition can be as diverse as the present one, while observing such technical limits, is a sign of the present vitality of the art of painting.

When an exhibition is predicated on the fact of diversity, as this exhibition is, the notion of a hierarchy in the arts becomes expendable; one can also dispense with some of the confidence in the universal status of art which former writers could express so cordially. The claim for art's universality usually involved its detachment from life and its contact with a realm above and beyond a changing world and the corruptible flesh. Now it is possible to value the artist not to the extent that he is the agent of a greater power (platonic essence or whatever), but to the extent that he is himself. When one faces a work of art, what is extra-ordinary is the fact of its creation. Heidegger, writing about Hölderlin, states: "The poems appear like a shrine without a temple, where what has been made into poetry is preserved".[14] The work embodies an order which is uniquely the concept of an individual artist and it is present in this form and no other form, because of the physical property of the materials worked. The artist reveals the capacity of an arbitrary system, a personally determined set of rules, to deliver a work of art. Because a system does not claim universal validity, it does not, therefore, become unsatisfactory or incomplete. On the contrary, we must accept, and work with the fact, that all human order, including that of the arts, is arbitrary. It follows that all systems and procedures adopted by artists are unlikely and improbable personal constructions and not, as was once believed approximations of superior order, emblems of stability.

If the starting point of any action has irreducible arbitrary elements (and in an age of almost total information about art, this is unavoidable), meaning may reside internally in the relation of the artist to the work. It is the logic with which one proceeds from the starting point and the power which one discovers in the process or working consistently that constitute the value of art. Say that one accepts an arbitrary limitation (one influenced by the confluence of the artist's personality and his time and place in history) on the way one will paint. What counts is the pursuit of the remaining possibilities with a clarity and intensity that would, in fact, have been impossible without the original restriction. The patience and invention that one brings to the chosen area, and not the correctness of the original premise, is what is moving and human in art.

Lawrence Alloway

NOTES

1. José Ortega y Gasset. "The Idea of the Generation", *Man and Crisis*, New York, Norton, 1962, p. 47.
2. Alfred P. Sloan, Jr. "My Years with General Motors, Pt. 1", *Fortune*, vol. 68, no. 3, 1963, p. 135.
3. Otto Benesch. *The Art of the Renaissance in Northern Europe*, Cambridge, Harvard University Press, 1945, pp. 42–47.
4. Mark Roskill, ed. *The Letters of Vincent Van Gogh*, New York, Atheneum, 1963. Letter dated mid-August, 1888, p. 277.
5. Corneille. "Rondom de Höstdstillingen", *Reflex 2*, n.d. [1948], unpaginated.
6. Asger Jorn. "Discours aux Pingouins", *Cobra*, Brussels, no. 1, 1948, p. 8.
7. Egill Jacobsen. "Introduktion til Carl Henning Pedersens Billeder", *Helhesten*, Copenhagen, vol. 1, no. 3, n.d. [c. 1942], pp. 73–75.
8. H. W. Janson. "After Betsy, What?", *Bulletin of the Atomic Scientists*, vol. 15, no. 2, 1959.
9. "Big Splash", *Time*, New York, May 18, 1959.
10. César Jannello. "Texture as a Visual Phenomenon", *Architectural Design*, London, vol. 33, no. 8, August 1963, pp. 394–396.
11. Henri Michaux, quoted by René Drouin. "De 1943 À 1958" in Juan Eduardo Cirlot, *La Peinture de Modest Cuixart*, Paris, 1958.
12. This theme is stressed by Gillian Feeley in her unpublished thesis *The Fantastic Element in the Art of Emil Nolde*, Cambridge, Radcliffe College, 1961.
13. According to Clement Greenberg ("The Crisis of the Easel Picture", *Art and Culture*, Boston, 1961) easel painting depends on a recessional space modelled in light and shade (à la Caravaggio). Hence, flat paintings must be *something else*. In point of fact, the easel painting, since its invention in the 16th century, has been the form of maximum freedom in the visual arts, the least constrained by patronage, the most conducive to experiment. Even the sensuality of means (whether gestural handling, intensity of color, or textural density), in which modern art abounds (even its alleged puritanical phases are sensationally intense) derives from the resources of easel painting. Tomás Maldonado (in *Max Bill*, Editorial Nueva Visión, Argentina, 1955, p. 18) put the matter succinctly: "The unity of visual arts must be envisaged as soon as possible, but without sacrificing to this end the particular media of expression—easel painting, sculpture, architecture—or adopting solutions which, though tempting, imply at this stage a technical and esthetic contradiction—mural painting, sculpture applied to architecture etc."
14. Martin Heidegger. *Existence and Being*, Chicago, Gateway, 1954, p. 234.

GUGGENHEIM INTERNATIONAL AWARD 1964

HORS CONCOURS: Miró as a previous Award winner is included *hors concours*. Paintings by Francis Bacon and Barnett Newman, at their own request, are reserved from consideration for the awards. Hans Hofmann's painting is added to the exhibition in respect for a distinguished artist on the Award Jury, and is, also, *hors concours*. These paintings are marked by an asterisk.

ARGENTINA 1. Ernesto Deira. SINCE ADAM AND EVE, 5. 1963. Oil and enamel on canvas, 77 x 100½".
Lent by Galeria Bonino, Buenos Aires.

2. José A. Fernández-Muro. BANNER. 1963. Oil and collage on canvas, 65 x 65".
Lent by Galeria Bonino, New York.

3. Rómulo Macció. TO LIVE: WITH A PURE HEART, 2. 1963. Enamel on canvas, 69 x 69".
Lent by Galeria Bonino, Buenos Aires.

4. Luis Felipe Noé. CHARISMA. 1963. Oil on canvas, 109½ x 77".
Lent by Galeria Bonino, Buenos Aires.

5. Jorge de la Vega. MUSIC HALL. 1963. Oil and collage on canvas, 100½ x 77".
Lent by Galeria Bonino, Buenos Aires.

AUSTRIA 6. Wolfgang Hollegha. PAINTING. 1963. Oil on canvas, 94¾ x 115⅝".
Lent by the artist.

7. Fritz Hundertwasser. 1000 WINDOWS. 1962.
Collection Julian J. and Joachim Jean Aberbach, New York.

8. Joseph Mikl. DARK FIGURE. 1961. Oil on canvas, 78½ x 66¾".
Lent by the artist.

9. Arnulf Rainer. GREEN OVER PAINTING. 1962. Oil on canvas, 71 x 51⅛".
Lent by the artist.

BELGIUM 10. Pierre Alechinsky. A THRONG OF LITTLE THINGS. 1962. Oil on canvas, 78¼ x 118".
Lent by the artist, courtesy of Lefebre Gallery, New York.

11. Paul Delvaux. THE NIGHT WATCHMAN, 2. 1961. Oil on board, 48 x 96".
Private Collection, New York.

12. René Magritte. THE WATERFALL. 1961. Oil on canvas, 31⅞ x 39⅜".
Lent by Alexander Iolas Gallery, New York.

CANADA 13. Graham Coughtry. TWO FIGURES, 9. 1963. Oil and lucite on canvas, 56 x 60".
Lent by The Isaacs Gallery, Toronto.

14. Guido Molinari. RED SPACE, 2. 1963. Oil on canvas, 63 x 58".
Lent by Jerrold Morris Gallery, Toronto.

15. Jean-Paul Riopelle. THE DANCE. 1962. Oil on canvas, 78⅞ x 78⅞".
Lent by Pierre Matisse Gallery, New York.

16. Terrence Syverson. UNTITLED. 1963. Oil on canvas, 102 x 108".
Lent by the artist.

CHILE 17. Matta. VERS L'UNI. 1963. Oil on canvas, 78¼ x 122″.
Lent by Galerie Daniel Cordier, Paris.

18. Ricardo Yrarrázaval. FIGURE (CHANGE 1). 1963. Oil on canvas, 57½ x 38″.
Lent by the artist.

CUBA 19. Wifredo Lam. TROPIC OF CAPRICORN. 1961. Oil on canvas, 58⅛ x 85″.
Collection Sonja Henie and Niels Onstad, Los Angeles.

DENMARK 20. Egill Jacobsen. LIMELIGHT. 1960. Oil on canvas, 73 x 43″.
Lent by Galerie K.-K., Copenhagen.

21. Asger Jorn. DEAD DRUNK DANES. 1960. Oil on canvas, 51 x 78¾″.
Collection Jon Nicholas Streep, New York.

22. Richard Mortensen. LORA. 1962. 63¼ x 51″.
Lent by Galerie Denise René, Paris.

23. Peter Nyborg. FAMILY. 1962. Oil on canvas, 83 x 70⅜″.
Lent by Galerie K.-K., Copenhagen.

24. Carl-Henning Pedersen. EUROPE. 1963. Tempera on canvas, 70¼ x 48¼″.
Lent by the artist.

FRANCE 25. Balthus. THE CUP OF COFFEE. 1960. Oil and gesso on canvas, 63¾ x 51″.
Lent by Pierre Matisse Gallery, New York.

26. Jean Dubuffet. PARIS—MONTPARNASSE. 1961. Oil on canvas, 66 x 88″.
Lent by Galerie Daniel Cordier, Paris.

27. Alain Jacquet. THE CHINESE TEMPLE (IMAGE D'ÉPINAL). 1961. Oil on canvas, 75⅝ x 88⅞″.
Lent by Galerie Breteau, Paris.

28. Marcel Pouget. THE SHREW. 1962. Oil on canvas, 76¾ x 51¼″.
Lent by the artist.

29. Victor de Vasarely. HELIOS. 1960. Oil on canvas, 72¼ x 86⅞″.
Lent by Galerie Denise René, Paris.

GERMANY 30. Horst Antes. COUPLE. 1962. Oil on canvas, 39⅜ x 39⅜″.
Lent by Galerie d'Eendt, Amsterdam.

31. Heinz Mack. CARDIOGRAM OF THE CYCLOPS. 1961-1962. Oil on canvas, 49⅜ x 43¼″.
Lent by Galerie Alfred Schmela, Dusseldorf.

32. Otto Piene. PINK FIRE FLOWER. 1963. Synthetic resin media on canvas, 47⅛ x 66¾″.
Lent by Galerie Alfred Schmela, Dusseldorf.

33. K. R. H. Sonderborg. THE BIG DOOR. 1962. Tempera on canvas, 52 x 65″.
Lent by Galerie Karl Flinker, Paris.

HUNGARY 34. Simon Hantaï. MARIALE AI. 1960. Oil on canvas, 88⅛ x 82⅛″.
Lent by Jean Fournier, Paris.

35. Judit Reigl. GREAT APPARITION. 1961. Oil on canvas, 69½ x 79½″.
Lent by Jean Fournier, Paris.

ISRAEL 36. Avshalom Okashi. ETERNAL NIGHT. 1963. Polyvinyl Acetate on canvas, 63 x 158″.
Lent by Galerie Israel, Tel Aviv.

37. Yecheskiel Streichman. JUDEAN LANDSCAPE. 1963. Oil on canvas, 79 x 78″.
Lent by Galerie Israel, Tel Aviv.

ITALY 38. Luigi Boillé. PAINTING. 1962. Oil on canvas, 78⅝ x 61″.
Lent by Galerie Stadler, Paris.

39. Giuseppe Capogrossi. SURFACE, 512. 1963. Oil on canvas, 79 x 118½″.
Lent by Galleria d'Arte del Naviglio, Milan.

40. Enrico Castellani. WHITE SURFACE, 2. 1962. Painted canvas and reliefs, 71 x 55″.
Lent by Galleria dell'Ariete, Milan.

41. Lucio Fontana. GREEN OVAL CONCEPT. 1963. Oil on canvas, 70 x 48½″.
Lent by Galleria dell'Ariete, Milan.

JAPAN 42. Minoru Kawabata. PAINTING, 2. 1963. Oil on canvas, 76⅜ x 102⅛″.
Lent by the artist.

43. Tomoyasu Murakami. WORK, 2. 1962. Japanese pigment color on paper, 45⅛ x 35⅛″.
Lent by Minami Gallery, Tokyo.

44. Toshinobu Onosato. PAINTING A. 1961-1962. Oil on canvas, 75¼ x 51″.
Lent by Minami Gallery, Tokyo.

45. Atsuko Tanaka. THANKS, SAM. 1963. Vinyl paint on canvas, 88¼ x 76⅛″.
Lent by Minami Gallery, Tokyo.

46. Jiro Yoshihara. PAINTING. 1963. Oil on canvas, 71⅛ x 89⅛″.
Lent by the artist.

MEXICO 47. Arnold Belkin. ROCK FIGURE. 1962. Oil on canvas, 66⅞ x 49½″.
Lent by The Zora Gallery, Los Angeles.

48. Francisco Icaza. MAN OF STONE. 1962. Oil on canvas, 74¾ x 57½″.
Lent by the artist.

49. David Alfaro Siqueiros. FLOWERS. 1962. Acrylic on cedar plywood, 18¼ x 15″.
Collection Tomás Marentes, Mexico City.

50. Rufino Tamayo. ROUTE TO TOWN. 1960. Oil on canvas, 20 x 14¼″.
Lent by M. Knoedler & Co., New York.

THE NETHERLANDS 51. Bram Bogart. DECOY COUNTRY. 1963. Mixed media on burlap on panel, 63¼ x 83¼″.
Lent by the artist.

52. Corneille. MEMORY OF SUMMER. 1961. Oil on canvas, 37 x 53″.
Collection Mr. and Mrs. Arnold Ginsburg, New York; courtesy Lefebre Gallery, New York.

53. Lucebert. GYPSIES. 1963. Oil on canvas, 57⅛ x 45¼″.
Lent by Marlborough, London.

54. Bram van Velde. COMPOSITION. 1962. Oil on canvas, 51 x 75¾″.
Lent by M. Knoedler & Co., Paris.

NORWAY 55. Gunnar Gundersen. COMPOSITION. 1962-1963. Acrylic on canvas, 33⅜ x 47⅞″.
Lent by the artist.

PERU 56. Fernando de Szyszlo. BLACK RAINBOW, 3. 1963. Oil on canvas, 61 x 61″.
Lent by the artist.

POLAND 57. Wojciech Fangor. BLACK WAVE. 1961. Oil on canvas, 79¼ x 47¼″.
Collection Beatrice and Hart Perry, New York.

SPAIN 58. Modest Cuixart. UNTITLED. 1961. Oil on canvas, 57½ x 44⅞″.
Collection Miss Isabelle Collin-Dufresne, New York.

*59. Joan Miró. BLUE II. 1961. Oil on canvas. 106¼ x 139¾″.
Lent by Pierre Matisse Gallery, New York.

60. Antonio Saura. UNTITLED. 1960-1961. Oil on canvas, 93½ x 74″.
Lent by Pierre Matisse Gallery, New York.

61. Antoni Tàpies. BIG WHITE HORIZONTAL. 1962. Synthetic resin on canvas, 77 x 122¼″.
Lent by Galerie Stadler, Paris.

SWEDEN 62. Olle Baertling. GARAK. 1962. Oil on canvas, 76⅞ x 38⅛″.
Lent by Galerie Denise René, Paris.

63. Öyvind Fahlström. DOCTOR LIVINGSTONE, I PRESUME. 1960-1961. Ink on canvas, 89¼ x 93¼″.
Lent by Galerie Daniel Cordier, Paris.

64. Evert Lundquist. THE URN. 1961. Oil on canvas, 45⅛ x 35″.
Lent by the artist.

SWITZERLAND 65. Max Bill. EXTENSION IN FOUR DIRECTIONS. 1961-1962. Oil on canvas, 75 x 75″.
Lent by the artist.

66. Alberto Giacometti. LARGE NUDE. 1962. Oil on canvas, 68¾ x 27½″.
Lent by Pierre Matisse Gallery, New York.

67. Vera Haller. TONDO, 2. 1963. Oil on canvas, diameter 62½″.
Lent by the artist.

68. Gottfried Honegger. TRIPTYCH. 1963. Oil on polyester, 39½ x 39½″ each.
Lent by Martha Jackson Gallery, New York.

69. Richard P. Lohse. 12 ASYMMETRICAL COLOR GROUPS WITH SYMMETRICAL CROSS FORM. 1962-1963.
Oil on canvas, 47⅛ x 47⅛″.
Lent by the artist.

UNITED KINGDOM * 70. Francis Bacon. NUDE. 1962. Oil on canvas, 78 x 56″.
Lent by Marlborough, London.

71. R. B. Kitaj. JUNTA. 1962. *including (from left to right)* What Thou Lovest Well Remains, The Rest is Dross
Born in Despotic
Dan Chatterton at Home
Old and New Tables (Doppelgänger) and
His Flower-Bedecked Bomb
Oil on canvas, 36 x 84″. Teratology.
Lent by the artist.

72. Henry Mundy. JU JU. 1962. Oil on board, 63 x 84″.
Lent by The Hanover Gallery, London.

73. Peter Stroud. RED CIRCUMVERT, 1. 1963. Emulsion on masonite, 60⅜ x 60¼″.
Lent by Marlborough, London.

74. William Turnbull. MANGO. 1963. Oil on canvas, 74 x 100¼″.
Lent by the artist.

UNITED STATES 75. Adolph Gottlieb. ROMAN THREE. 1962. Oil on canvas, 78⅛ x 66⅛″.
Lent by the artist.

76. Philip Guston. UNTITLED. 1962. Oil on canvas, 68 x 78″.
Lent by the artist.

77. Willem de Kooning. UNTITLED. 1963. Oil on canvas, 80 x 70″.
Joseph H. Hirshhorn Collection, New York.

78. Robert Motherwell. ELEGY TO THE SPANISH REPUBLIC, 70. 1961. Oil on canvas, 69 x 114″.
Lent by the artist; courtesy Marlborough, New York.

* 79. Barnett Newman. THE THIRD. 1962. Oil on canvas, 101 x 121¼″.
Lent by the artist.

VENEZUELA 80. Jacobo Borges. LET'S ALL GO TO THE FIESTA. 1962. Oil on canvas, 62¼ x 80¼″.
Collection Museo de Bellas Artes, Caracas.

81. Alejandro Otero. COLORHYTHM, 62. 1960. Lacquer on wood, 78¼ x 21⅛″.
Collection Museo de Bellas Artes, Caracas.

ADDITIONAL* 82. Hans Hofmann. COLOR BALLET. 1961. Oil on canvas, 78 x 84″.
Lent by Samuel M. Kootz Gallery Inc., New York.

79. Barnett Newman. *The Third*. 1962.

75. Adolph Gottlieb. *Roman Three.* 1962.

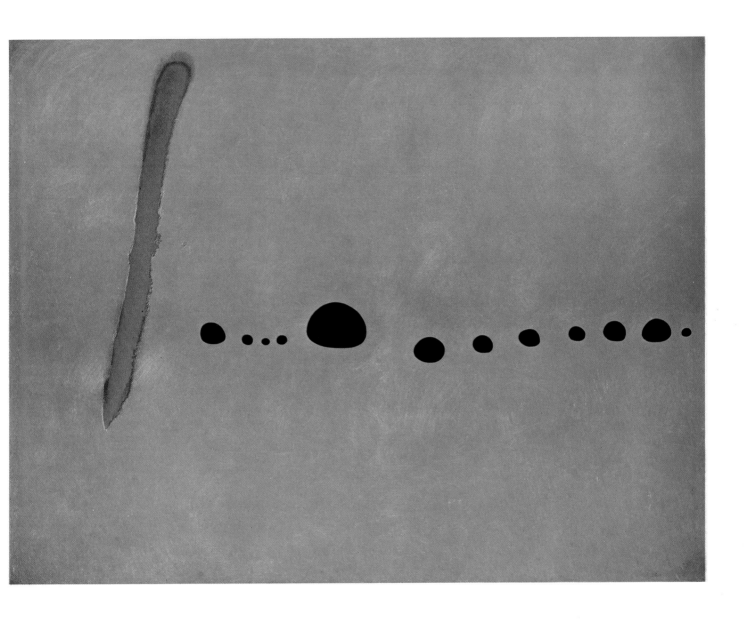

59. Joan Miró. *Blue, 2.* 1961.

43. Tomoyasu Murakami. *Work, 2.* 1962. (above)   9. Arnulf Rainer. *Green Over Painting.* 1962. (below)

36. Avshalom Okashi. *Eternal Night.* 1963.

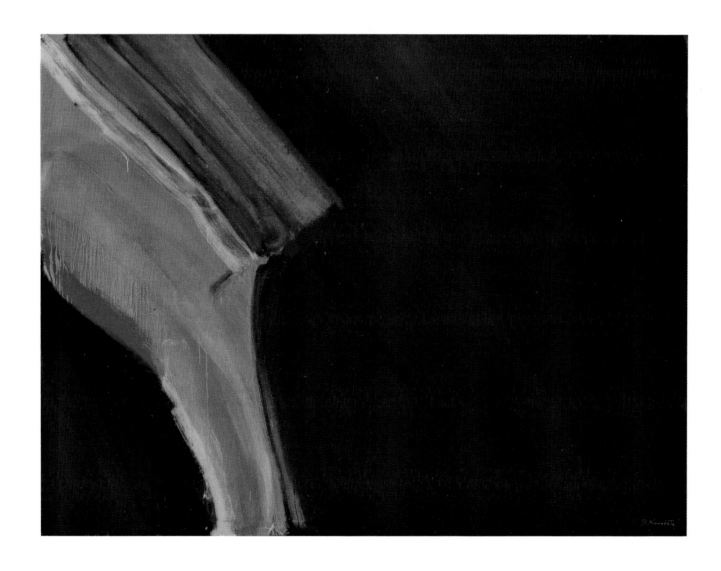

42. Minoru Kawabata. *Painting, 2.* 1963.

74. William Turnbull. *Mango.* 1963.

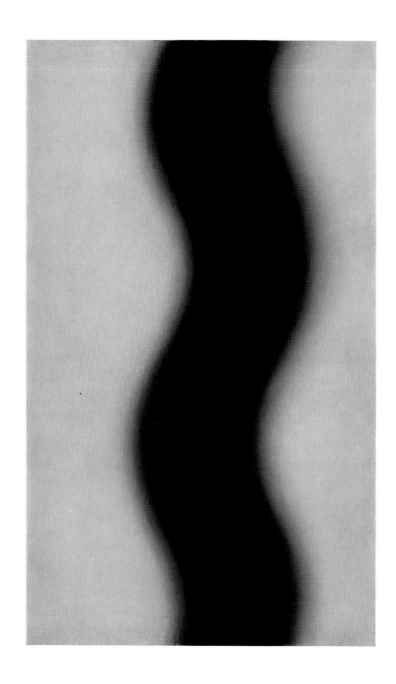

57. Wojciech Fangor. *Black Wave*. 1961.

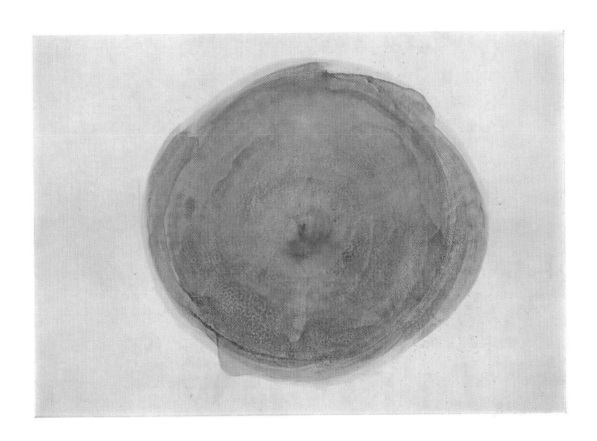

32. Otto Piene. *Pink Fire Flower*. 1963.

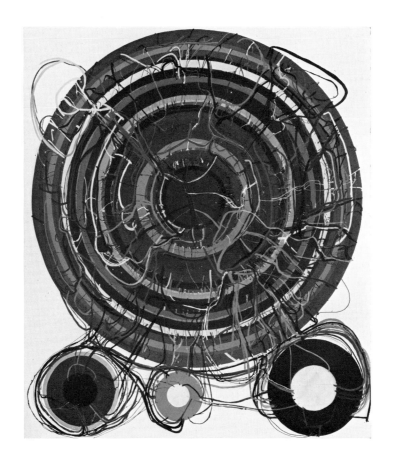

45. Atsuko Tanaka. *Thanks, Sam.* 1963. (above)   16. Terrence Syverson. *Untitled.* 1963. (below)

46. Jiro Yoshihara. *Painting.* 1963.

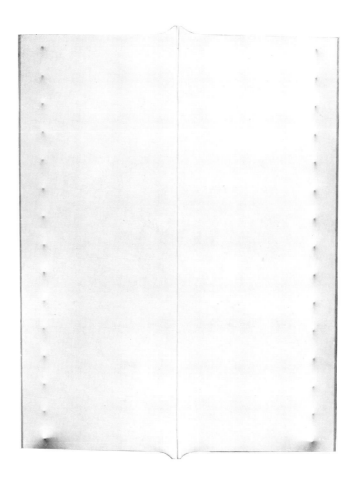

40. Enrico Castellani. *White Surface, 2.* 1962. (above)　　　　39. Giuseppe Capogrossi. *Surface, 512.* 1963. (below)

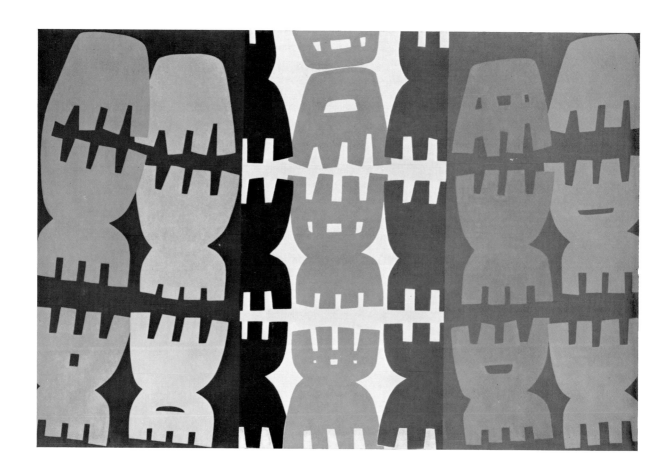

41. Lucio Fontana. *Green Oval Concept.* 1963.

14. Guido Molinari. *Red Space, 2.* 1963. (above)   73. Peter Stroud. *Red Circumvert, 1.* 1963 (below)

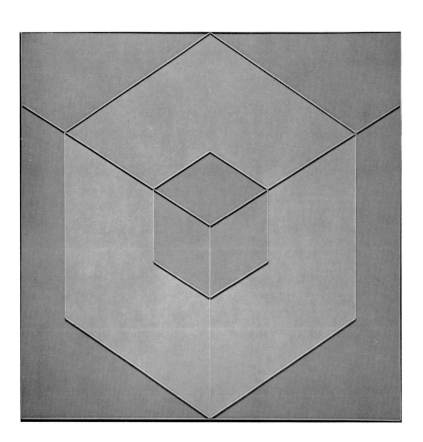

65. Max Bill. *Extension in Four Directions*. 1961–1962.

69. Richard P. Lohse. *12 Asymmetrical Color Groups with Symmetrical Cross Form.* 1962–1963. (above)   44. Toshinobu Onosato. *Painting A.* 1961–1962. (bel...

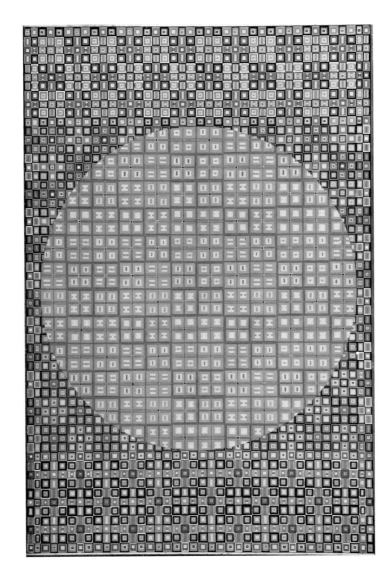

29. Victor de Vasarely. *Helios.* 1960.

22. Richard Mortensen. *Lora*. 1962. (above)

68. Gottfried Honegger. *Triptych*. 1963. (below)

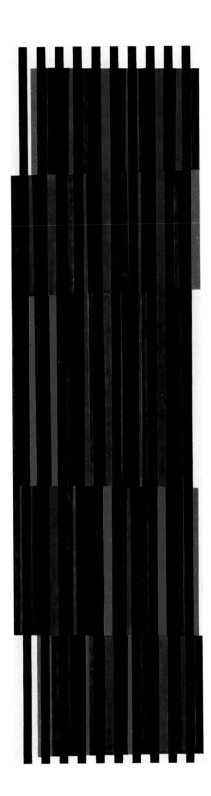

81. Alejandro Otero. *Colorhythm, 62.* 1960.

55. Gunnar Gundersen. *Composition*. 1962–1963.

62. Olle Baertling. *Garak*. 1962.

33. K. R. H. Sonderborg. *The Big Door*. 1962. (above)

2. José A. Fernandez-Muro. *Banner*. 1963. (below)

61. Antoni Tàpies. *Big White Horizontal*. 1962.

34. Simon Hantaï. *Mariale AI*. 1960. (above)　　　31. Heinz Mack. *Cardiogram of the Cyclops*. 1961–1962. (below)

27. Alain Jacquet. *The Chinese Temple (Image D'Épinal)*. 1961. (above)   38. Luigi Boillé. *Painting*. 1962. (below)

58. Modest Cuixart. *Untitled*. 1961. (above)   64. Evert Lundquist. *The Urn*. 1961. (below)

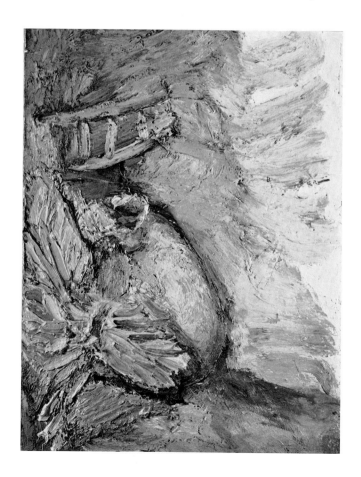

51. Bram Bogart. *Decoy Country*. 1963. (above)   13. Graham Coughtry. *Two Figures, 8*. 1963. (below)

78. Robert Motherwell. *Elegy to the Spanish Republic, 70.* 1961.

77. Willem de Kooning. *Untitled*. 1963.

76. Philip Guston. *Untitled*. 1962.

15. Jean-Paul Riopelle. *The Dance*. 1962.

82. Hans Hofmann. *Color Ballet*. 1961. (above)　　　67. Vera Haller. *Tondo, 2*. 1963 (below)

8. Joseph Mikl. *Dark Figure*. 1961. (above)   37. Yecheskiel Streichman. *Judean Landscape*. 1963. (below)

6. Wolfgang Hollegha. *Painting*. 1963.

35. Judit Reigl. *Great Apparition*. 1961.

21. Asger Jorn. *Dead Drunk Danes.* 1960.

24. Carl-Henning Pedersen. *Europe*. 1963. (above)   10. Pierre Alechinsky. *A Throng of Little Things*. 1962. (below)

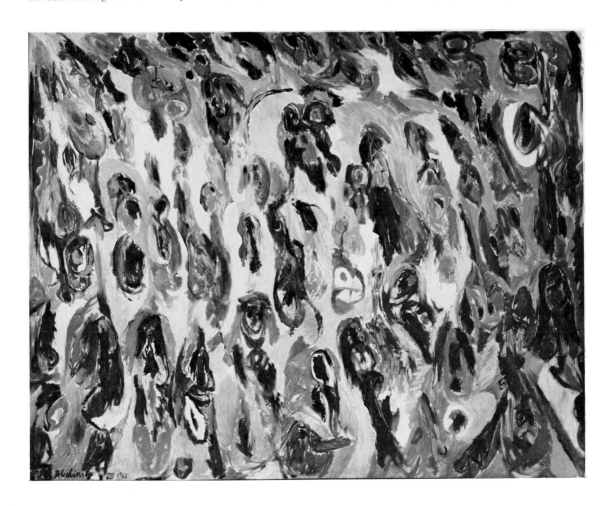

20. Egill Jacobsen. *Limelight*. 1960. (above)

52. Corneille. *Memory of Summer*. 1961. (below)

48. Francisco Icaza. *Man of Stone*. 1962. (above)　　　　　47. Arnold Belkin. *Rock Figure*. 1962. (below)

56. Fernando de Szyszlo. *Black Rainbow, 3*. 1963.

50. Rufino Tamayo. *Route to Town*. 1960. (above)　　　18. Ricardo Yrarrázaval. *Figure (Change 1)*. 1963. (below)

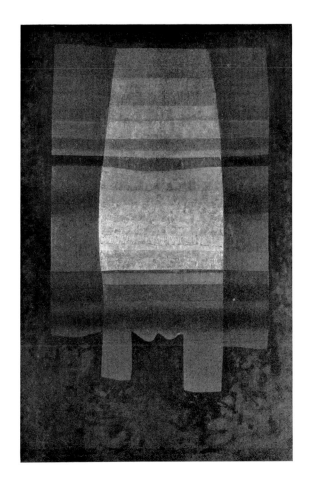

54. Bram van Velde. *Composition*. 1962.

72. Henry Mundy. *Ju Ju*. 1962.

26. Jean Dubuffet. *Paris-Montparnasse.* 1961.

19. Wifredo Lam. *Tropic of Capricorn.* 1961.

53. Lucebert. *Gypsies.* 1963. (above)　　　　30. Horst Antes. *Couple.* 1962. (below)

28. Marcel Pouget. *The Shrew*. 1962. (above)   23. Peter Nyborg. *Family*. 1962. (below)

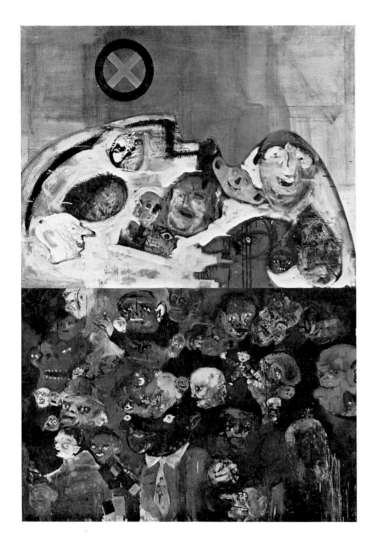

4. Luis Felipe Noé. *Charisma.* 1963.

5. Jorge de la Vega. *Music Hall.* 1963.

1. Ernesto Deira. *Since Adam and Eve, 5.* 1963.

80. Jacobo Borges. *Let's All Go to the Fiesta*. 1962. (above)   60. Antonio Saura. *Untitled*. 1960–1961. (below)

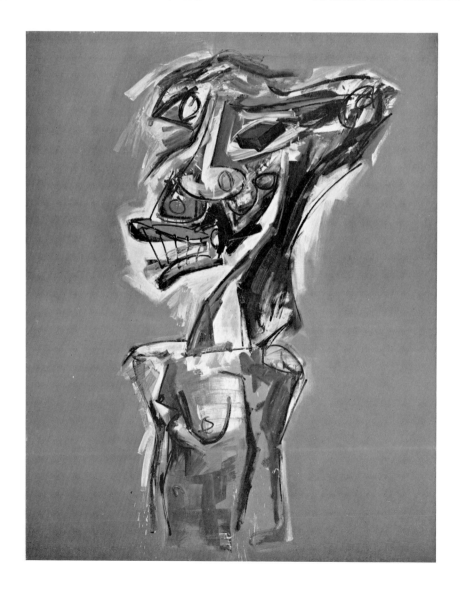

3. Rómulo Macció. *To Live: With a Pure Heart*, 2. 1963.

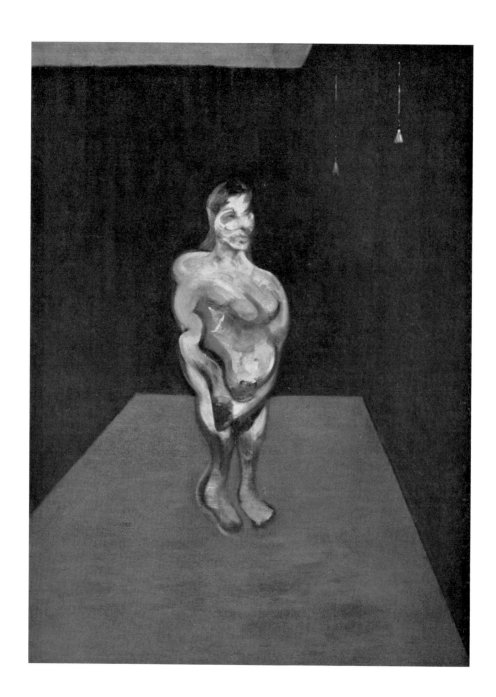

70. Francis Bacon. *Nude*. 1962.

66. Alberto Giacometti. *Large Nude*. 1962.

25. Balthus. *The Cup of Coffee.* 1960.

7. Fritz Hundertwasser. *1,000 Windows.* 1962. (above)

71. R. B. Kitaj. *Junta.* 1962. (below)

63. Öyvind Fahlström. *Doctor Livingstone, I Presume.* 1960–1961.

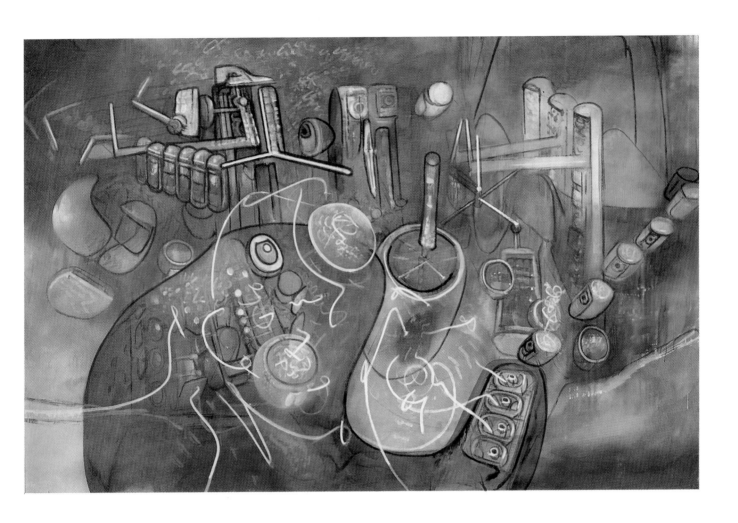

17. Matta. *Vers L'Uni*. 1963.

11. Paul Delvaux. *The Night Watchman, 2.* 1961.

12. René Magritte. *The Waterfall*. 1961.

49. David Alfaro Siqueiros. *Flowers*. 1962.

DOCUMENTATION

ANTHOLOGY

A random selection of complete texts or selected quotations from the rich store of writings by artists in the present exhibition.

BARNETT NEWMAN

THE FIRST MAN WAS AN ARTIST

A scientist has just caught the tail of another metaphor. Out of the Chinese dragon's teeth, piled high in harvest on the shelves of Shanghai's drugstores and deep in the Java mud, a half million years old, he has constructed Meganthropus palaeojavanicus, "man the great," the giant, who, the paleontologists now tell us, was our human ancestor. And for many, he has become more real than Cyclops, than the Giant of the Beanstalk. Those unconvinced by the poetic dream, who reject the child's fable, are now sure of a truth found today 500,000 years old. Shall we artists quarrel with those who need to wait for the weights of scientific proof to believe in poetry? Or shall we let them enjoy their high adventure laid out in mud and in drugstore teeth? For truth is for them at last the Truth.

Quarrel we must, for there is the implication in this paleontological find of another attempt to claim possession of the poetic gesture; that the scientist rather than the artist discovered the Giant. It is not enough for the artist to announce with arrogance his invincible position: that the job of the artist is not to discover truth, but to fashion it, that the artist's work was done long ago. This position, superior as it may be, separates the artist from everyone else, declares his role against that of all. The quarrel here must include a critique of paleontology, an examination of the new sciences.

In the last sixty years, we have seen mushroom a vast cloud of "sciences" in the fields of culture, history, philosophy, psychology, economics, politics, aesthetics, in an ambitious attempt to claim the non-material world. Why the invasion? Is it out of fear that its materialistic interpretation of physical phenomena, its narrow realm of physics and chemistry, may give science a minor historical position if, in the larger attempt to resolve the metaphysical mysteries, the physical world may take only a small place? Has science, in its attempt to dominate all realms of thought, been driven willy nilly to act politically so that, by denying any place to the metaphysical world, it could give its own base of operations a sense of security? Like any state or church, science found the drive to conquer necessary to protect the security of its own state of physics. To accomplish this expansion, the scientist abandoned the revolutionary scientific act for a theological way of life.

The domination of science over the mind of modern man has been accomplished by the simple tactic of ignoring the prime scientific quest; the concern with its original question *what?* When it was found that the use of this question to explore all knowledge was utopian, the scientist switched from an insistence on it to a roving position of using any question. It was easy for him to do so because he could thrive on the grip mathematical discipline had, as a romantic symbol of purity and perfection, on the mind of man. So intense is the reverence for this symbol, scientific method, that it has become the new theology. And the mechanics of this theology, so brilliant is the rhythm of its logic-rite, its identification of truth with proof, that it has overwhelmed the original ecstasy of scientific quest, scientific inquiry.

For there is a difference between method and inquiry. Scientific inquiry, from its beginnings, has perpetually asked a single and specific question, *what?* What is the rainbow, what is an atom, what a star? In the pursuit of this question, the physical sciences have built a realm of thought that has validity because the question is basic for the attainment of descriptive knowledge and permits a proper integration between its quest, the question *what* constantly maintained, and its tool, mathematics or logic, for the discovery of its answer. Scientific method, however, is free of the question. It can function on any question, or, as in mathematics, without a question. But the choice of quest, the kind of question, is the basis of the scientific act. That is why it is so pathetic to watch the scientist, so proud of his critical acumen, delude himself by the splendor of the ritual of method which, concerned only with its own relentless ceremonial dance, casts its spell not only over the lay observer but also over the participating scientist, with its incessant drumbeat of proof.

Original man, what does it matter who he was, giant or pygmy? What was he? That is the question for a science of paleontology that would have meaning for us today. For if we knew what original man was, we could declare what today's man is not. Paleontology, by building a sentimental science around the question *who* (who was your great-grandfather), cannot be excused for substituting this question for the real one, because, according to the articles of faith that make up scientific method, there is not nor can there ever be sufficient proof for positive answer. After all, paleontology, like the other non-material sciences, has entered a realm where the only questions worth discussing are the questions that cannot be proved. We cannot excuse the abdication of its primal scientific responsibility because paleontology substituted the sentimental question *who* for the scientific *what*. Who cares who he was? What was the first man, was he a hunter, a toolmaker, a farmer, a worker, a priest, or a politician? Undoubtedly the first man was an artist.

A science of paleontology that sets forth this proposition can be written if it builds on the postulate that the aesthetic act always precedes the social one. The totemic act of wonder in front of the tiger-ancestor came before the act of murder. It is important to keep in mind that the necessity for dream is stronger than any utilitarian need. In the language of science, the necessity for understanding the unknowable comes before any desire to discover the unknown.

Man's first expression, like his first dream, was an aesthetic one. Speech was a poetic outcry rather than a demand for communication. Original man, shouting his consonants, did so in yells of awe and anger at his tragic state, at his own self-awareness and at his own helplessness before the void. Philologists and semioticians are beginning to accept the concept that, if language is to be defined as the ability to communicate by means of signs, be they sounds or gestures, then language is an animal power. Anyone who has watched the common pigeon circle his female knows that she knows what he wants.

The human in language is literature, not communication. Man's first cry was a song. Man's first address to a neighbor was a cry of power and solemn weakness, not a request for a drink of water. Even the animal makes a futile attempt at poetry. Ornithologists explain the cock's crow as an ecstatic outburst of his power. The loon gliding lonesome over the lake, with whom is he communicating? The dog, alone, howls at the moon. Are we to say that the first man called the sun and the stars *God* as an act of communication and only after he had finished his day's labor? The myth came before the hunt. The purpose of man's first speech was an address to the unknowable. His behavior had its origin in his artistic nature.

Just as man's first speech was poetic before it became utilitarian, so man first built an idol of mud before he fashioned an axe. Man's hand traced the stick through the mud to make a line before he learned to throw the stick as a javelin. Archeologists tell us that the ax-head suggested the ax-head idol. Both are found in the same strata so they must have been contemporaneous. True, perhaps, that the ax-head idol of stone could not have been carved without axe instruments, but this is a division in metier, not in time, since the mud figure anticipated both the stone figure and the axe. (A figure can be made out of mud but an axe cannot.) The God image, not pottery, was the first manual act. It is the materialistic corruption of present-day anthropology that has tried to make men believe that original man fashioned pottery before he made sculpture. Pottery is the product of civilization. The artistic act is man's personal birthright.

The earliest written history of human desires proves that the meaning of the world cannot be found in the social act. An examination of the first chapter of Genesis offers a better key to the human dream. It was inconceivable to the archaic writer that original man, that Adam, was put on earth to be a toiler, to be a social animal. The writer's creative impulses told him that man's origin was that of an artist and he set him up in a Garden of Eden close to the Tree of Knowledge, of right and wrong, in the highest sense of divine revelation. The fall of man was understood by the writer and his audience not as a fall from Utopia to struggle, as the sociologicians would have it, nor, as the religionists would have us believe, as a fall from Grace to Sin, but rather that Adam, by eating from the Tree of Knowledge, sought the creative life to be, like God, "a creator of worlds," to use Rashi's phrase, and was reduced to the life of toil only as a result of a jealous punishment.

In our inability to live the life of a creator can be found the meaning of the fall of man. It was a fall from the good, rather than from the abundant, life. And it is precisely here that the artist today is striving for a closer approach to the truth concerning original man than can be claimed by the paleontologist, for it is the poet and the artist who are concerned with the function of original man and who are trying to arrive at his creative state. What is the *raison d'etre*, what is the explanation of the seemingly insane drive of man to be painter and poet if it is not an act of defiance against man's fall and an assertion that he return to the Adam of the Garden of Eden? For the artists are the first men.

TIGER'S EYE, Westport, Connecticut, No. 1, 1947

ROBERT MOTHERWELL

A. ELEGIES (To The Spanish Republic)

The Spanish "Elegies" are an effort to symbolize a subjective image of modern Spain. They are all in black and white: they are funeral pictures, laments, dirges, elegies—barbaric and austere.

B. CAPRICCIOS

The word "Capriccio" is used as by musicians, to mean a "composition in a more or less free form," often fantastic. The subjects are the classical ones of 20th Century Parisian abstract painting: figures, interiors, still lifes. The fantasy is brutal and ironical.

C. WALL PAINTINGS

The "Wall Paintings" are not conceived of as easel paintings but as enhancements of a wall, and so called; and their subject is not an image, whether subjective or "real", but the culture of modern painting. The projected mural (listed as Number 7) for the Attleboro school designed by Walter Gropius and his partners in the Architects Collaborative, for example, does not have sports, or some other "teen-age" pre-occupation as a subject, but simply the character of a wall painted with style.

Kootz Gallery, New York,
November 14–December 4, 1950, *Motherwell*

Motherwell, *At Five in the Afternoon*, 1949.

AT FIVE IN THE AFTERNOON, 1949

A Line of Garcia Lorca. The painting is part of a series of Spanish Elegies (about 80 Elegies altogether). One reason I changed the name of the series as a whole to *Elegy to the Spanish Republic* was that someone occasionally would come up to me and say I saw a most marvellous picture by you—what was the name? Something to do with cocktails.

I take an elegy to be a funeral lamentation or funeral song for something one cared about. The Spanish Elegies are not political but my private insistence that a terrible death happened that should not be forgot. They are as eloquent as I could make them. But the pictures are also general metaphors of the contrast between life and death, and their interrelation.

Smith College Museum of Art, Northampton,
January 10–28, 1963, *Robert Motherwell*

WILLIAM TURNBULL

HEAD SEMANTICS, 1960

From about 50-56 I titled a number of paintings and sculptures "HEAD". The word meant for me what I imagined the word "Landscape" had meant for some painters—a format that could carry different loadings.

Almost anything could be a head—and a head almost anything—given the slightest clue to the decoding.

The shape basic to most of them relates about as much to a head as that lumpy sphere that crowns every snowman.

In the sculptures I wanted to get rid of amputations across the chest (which is always how I've felt about "portrait busts") and in the paintings I didn't want to "transpose a head from three-dimensional reality to a flat surface"—but to imagine what a head would be if flat (squeezed between two pieces of glass like a micro slide) and made of paint marks.

The sort of thing that interested me was—
how little will suggest a head
how much load will the shape take and still read head
head as colony
head as landscape
head as mask
head as ideogram
head as sign, etc.

A few years ago I dropped the head image. In the paintings I still use a circle or sections of it, and with sculpture, because the forms often sit on top of column-like shapes, they still often read as heads.
1960

I'd like to be able to make one saturated field of colour, so that you wouldn't feel you were short of all the others.

UPPERCASE, London, No. 4, n.d. [1960]

What is the nearest we have come to the equivalent of a temple or shrine in this century (and *of* this century)? The closest I have got to this experience has been the large exhibitions of Pollock or Rothko; the Monets in the Tuilleries (the Nymphéas); and especially the late Matisses exhibited in the Museum of Modern Art, New York. These were for me an experience close to the exaltation of the sacred, a ritual of celebration which avoided the guilt of the Crucifixion or the blood of sacrifice which I often associate with such sensations. Is it a desire to create environmental experiences of this sort that makes some artist prefer personal exhibitions, and find group showing unsatisfactory? It is with some such idea in mind that I work.

LIVING ARTS, London, no. 1, 1963, p. 15

HENRY MUNDY

EFFECTS USED IN PAINTING

Taut and loose, a scrabble of lines of various thickness together with carefully ruled ones.

Preliminary marks veiled by thin washes, sudden impact of opaque lacquer. The feeling of old lumber in a white marble interior.

Lines. Ruled, scratched, rubbed, scrawled, with graphite, with a knife, with a soft brush.

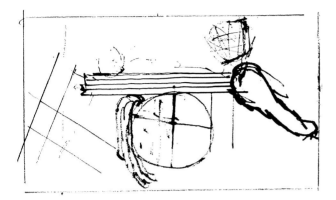

Mundy, *Sketch*, 1961

Ambiguity. It is not a landscape with square stones, one of the rectangles is matte and paper-thin. The telegraph-pole thing is absurdly huge and stubby for its neat set of wires embedded in crockery and pencil scribble.

A disc is a corroded compass made of "nursery blue".

GAZETTE, London, no. 2, 1961

OTTO PIENE

DARKNESS AND LIGHT

It is curious that in so many branches of art today darkness plays such a large part. All the more so since one spends the greater part of one's life, the waking part, in light. One "turns on" the light to prolong that part. All this seems to affect theatre, opera, film and painting very little. The painters now a la mode cover ever greater areas with black. The spectator at the opera or at a play sits in a huge dark room with a little light at one end, in which shadowy figures move. Night is the classical time for dramatic events, especially tragic ones. It is the favorite time for those who have the feeling for it. Then they can accomplish their tremendous deeds, then they can communicate their intoxicating experiences. Still, one must admit that the deep blue of night is different again from the stifling blackness, the loss of feeling and direction which arise[s] when the invisible is dragged into sight.

Blackness in works of art is of two kinds: on the one hand it can be a sign, a symbol as in writing; on the other it can be the expression of desire for a colour-space. In the first case the black is the medium which makes the symbol visible and as such is justified, so long as the symbol itself has validity. In the second case, which one meets with repeatedly in recent years, the black is intended to express menace and mystery, the daemonic secret which is only guessed at. Black—like all dark colours, tends to become the expression of the invisible as such. But the invisible element which is of interest in such works of art is that aspect of the human spirit which cannot be directly known, its invisible part so to speak. It is this aspect which occupies the psychologists. In short, darkness in art is a result of that fatal psychologising which is becoming ever more widely spread. It is surely atavistic to maintain that darkness is mysterious, but not light. I myself find it natural to use the effect of darkness just so far as it serves to make lightness lighter, that is to say more distinct, to phrase it like a tone in music, rendering its nuances perceptible. The contrast is the barbarian roar which, coming from nowhere, is most terrifying in the night. Light has the strength and continuity of the human pulse, and the breath of its subtle vibration can grow to amazing violence. Light is for us the incarnation of life itself. It is the flirtation with death and the death wish which attracts the artist to the sphere of darkness and of night. I believe that pictures should be light and luminous. Destruction, annihilation, decay, the dying of the dust, these are things which we all have seen. To call them up continually seems to me like the sympathetic magic of the bull on the cave wall. Are we still as we were fifty thousand years ago? Is the art of darkness trying to persuade us that drama, tragic conflict—regrettable as the end may be, are the normal course? It is just as possible to say: how strong (and how beautiful) is a colour of true luminosity. And those great houses in which theatre and opera play and films are shown, could they not try to light more than the wretched bit of stage or screen: Should they not reflect (or consider proposals) how to achieve a complete fulfillment of space for what they have to offer? Probably, though this would mean the abandonment of their favorite subject, man tormenting himself. But at the moment it seems to me a most questionable undertaking to play on people's willing habits to tempt them into the darkness. Would not sleep be of more use to them? Not to speak of the spaceless space, the visible infinity of the luminous blue night, to which we give our deepest reverence because it possesses the pure beauty of passivity. But the space of action and movement, of life itself, is still that of light. Darkness and gloom are the expression of men who themselves are gloomy and dark. Darkness is the false absolute, black and without degree. Lightness is the continuum, subject in itself to continuous change, therefore perceptible and a continual stimulus.

To wake or to sleep?
Wake to sleep or sleep to wake?
Sleeping or waking?

AZIMUTH, Milan, no. 2, January, 1960

WHAT IS A PAINTING?

The painting is a field of force, an arena in which the artist's energies encounter melted, poured movements of color, welcomed from the universe's profusion, guided capillarily in the spectator's open soul.

WHAT IS COLOR?

Color is the articulation of light.

WHAT IS LIGHT?

Light is the domain of all lives, the element of man and image and man, captured, gathered, intensified in the vibration that has seized the artist, the painting, and the spectator.

WHAT IS VIBRATION?

Vibration is the nuance which becomes alive, which forbids the contrast, disgraces tragedy, dismisses drama; it is the vehicle of frequency, the blood of color, the pulse of light, the pure emotion, the purity of image, pure energy.

WHAT IS PURE ENERGY?

It is pure continuity, the perpetuity, the inextinguishability of life.

What is all this, image, light, vibration, pure energy? Life. Life in freedom.

10 TEXTE, Nota Galerie, March 1961, M

ENRICO CASTELLANI

TOTALITY IN THE ART OF TODAY

Ever new attributes are coined and applied to contemporary art by well-wishing people with the scope of making it better known and better understood; but these people, however, both because of their origins and their significance are the least adapted to define today's art and they are even capable of sublimating one aspect of it to the detriment of the unitary whole. They are, therefore, a source of confusion.

To speak of monochrome art means, in fact, giving great importance to the external aspect of motion, which is in no way a form of aestheticism, forgetting the historical significance, which cannot be repeated in time; it also means making the error of convalidating any surface painted with a single colour of a bas-relief or graphited plaster, even when at the origin of these manifestations nothing exists other than the enlargement of a splash of colour to the margins of the canvas or a badly disguised impressionistic naturalism or even a rhetorical, ecclesiastical existentialism. This error has already been made, and there exists today an academy of monochrome art; just exactly as happened in 1925, when everyone discovered that he was making splashes, today everyone insists on having painted completely white or blue or red canvases in 1940.

The truth is that monochromatic painting offered the last opportunity to painting in general to differentiate itself from the other arts. The surface, which previously had served to describe, hint at or suggest, and which was the scene of idylls, dramas or even idle talk, is not mute. A monochrome curtain has fallen on the last act of painting, and it would be useless now to indulge in mystical contemplation. An analogous discourse could be undertaken as regards the partial truths which, from time to time—and often simultaneously with some retarded discovery of a greatly heeded critic—seem to obtain attention up to the point of being the subjects of seductive theories which pretend to be total and definitive as regards art.

It is agreed upon that motion is a particular prerogative of contemporary art and that structure is an essential element of movement, but to differentiate it signifies falling into the anecdotal, and motion becomes figurative and illusory, and time remains extraneous. On the other hand, in the place of any virtual volume I prefer the motor which moves nothing but, being well-balanced, is the animated object vibrant with power. An ugly painting launched at supersonic speed remains what it is and rapidly disappears from sight; a work, instead, which exists in virtue of physical motion reverses the terms of our problem because, by making use of the scenographic procedure, it tends to give an artificial rhythm to time and, therefore, to falsify its entity. And exactly at that point is where we give it importance as a means of communication.

In fact, we are less impressed by the work in and of itself than by its relationship historically with the sum of experiences and necessities surrounding us. It is in this sense that I like to define myself as a realist opposed to the rhetorical defenders of an eternally unchangeable reality and to the esthetes of para-scientific formulae.

The surface of my canvases or of my laminated plastics or of other materials—plastically dematerialized by the lack of color—tend to modulate, to the extent that they are a compositional element, and accept the third dimension which renders them perceptible. Light is an instrument of this perception at this point. Contingent forms and intensities are here abandoned in their accidentality. But since these surfaces are no longer part of the domain of painting or sculpture and since they are able to assume the monumental character of architecture and to redimension space

they are the reflection of the total interior space, free of contradictions, which we are searching for and, therefore, they exist to the extent that they are objects of instantaneous assimilation and have the duration of an act of communion prior to being confined by time in their material precariousness.

ZERO, Dusseldorf, no. 3, 1963

Alechinsky, *Study in the Morphology of Orange Peels*, 1962

CARL-HENNING PEDERSEN

ABSTRACT ART OR IMAGINARY ART—AN ARTIST'S WORK

It is not really possible to associate the word "abstract" with painting, even when the picture does not use recognizable objects, with the expression of color and the sensitivity of the lines. What all artists called "abstract" have in common is that they are working from the world of unlimited imagination. Every artist's work will be different, as different as human beings are one from another. A better collective term for this form of art is "imaginary art"; such a term would straightaway explain what it is all about. It would show the relationship to primitive and oriental art, as well as to the free activity of expression in children. It would also show the flow and inspiration of modern art. As long as the word "abstract" is used, people will think that the artist has discovered a new artistic language which they are not qualified to understand. They believe that it is something they have to learn and do not see that "imaginary art" is based on a central idea in the human being, something which can be perceived and sensed by all without previous knowledge or understanding: something which they themselves experienced as children, but forgot once they thought they had to act as adults and follow the mediocre traditions of society.

There are no limits to an artist's world of color. Any human feeling may be written into color. A human being's whole personality is reflected in his handwriting. The line tells everything. In a painting, color and shape are united and disclose the artist and his world of emotion to the spectator. One must seek in order to find, otherwise it is only a coincidence if one finds what is important.

In the process of creating a painting, one leaps into the air from a certain point before falling back, and when attempting the next jump tries to make an even better leap, to reach even further out. And so it continues, always starting from the beginning. Barely noticeably, the starting point is gradually moved, but one feels as though one is still leaping from the same spot. It is the same for everyone. No one is so great that he does not have to leap again and again. Those who cheat are disqualified from the start. It does not really matter who makes the big jumps and who makes the small ones as long as one continues to leap and make the attempt; this is what makes the great big leap. The attempts of the various artists differ, some are more careful, others throw themselves out spontaneously just to see what happens.

The results are judged according to what the individual puts into it: this is what is significant. Some manage to put more into it, but all are important. Naturally, some are influenced and inspired by others, but such is life. It is one big pattern of relationships continuously rubbing against each other, segregating the undesirable elements in the process. Apparently "imaginary art" has a common language, created by common effort, but this is superficial. A round sun, or just a round shape has been used by all painters. But this shape is so primeval in origin, and of such vital symbolic character in contrast to the erected shape that it must be included by all who work out from their imagination. Herein lies the difference between painting that depicts something, which is naturalism in its purest form, and imaginary art. Necessity dictates rhythmic and emotional laws in a painting which can best be followed by working freely from the imagination.

If you wish to create a painting that is as free as possible, why not remain within the confines of pure painting? A painting with no recognizable objects? Why do some of you fill up your pictures with imaginary beings, human as well as animal? Because pictures are also magic, in the new sense of the word. A person expresses himself to others in the language of the senses and formulates his message in a certain way; a magic character who catches the eyes of others and silently shouts of its presence, or manifests itself so peacefully that it seeps out into the atmosphere. Magic is an invocation, and even though we do not need to invoke good or evil, this power lies behind everything. The world around us crowds in to create experiences which are thus developed materially. It is not so strange that the artist in his imagination must devote himself to other beings surrounding him and that these beings are re-created in his imagination. The human being has never looked like that. Not even the artist has ever seen him until he appears vividly on the canvas, created out of line and color. But nothing comes from nothing. There is a force or power that drives everything and this, more than anything else, is shown by the individual's artistic creation. The fundamental nature of art has remained unchanged for many thousands of years. At least that is the way we feel. And yet the same problems are presented in a new fashion and each generation produces its own solutions.

Probably the strongest artistic expression comes into being when the work is created spontaneously. The picture is developed quickly. The stirring of the mind is read clearly in the painting and gives the spectator a better opportunity to acquaint himself with the personality of the painter and what he has intended to put into the picture. Spontaneity is movement which stems from the innermost depths of a person.

Every artist has his own method of approaching his work.

But by and large it is the same for everyone. It is artistically enriching to feel that others are expressing themselves in the language of the senses and to perceive the creations of men which took place many years ago. One by one they are cooperating in building up the kingdom of art through the ages.

There are many who paint in order to please; they borrow others' clothes and pretend that they are their own and wear them out completely. Protests should be made against such persons. They are of no great importance in the long run, but they do steal people's good will and serve them with bad food. Unfortunately, they are many inferior cooks among artists. They do not need to be so, nobody does, although not everyone can leap equally far. Perhaps it is because the painting has to be sold for the artist to exist. Involuntarily he becomes like any other manufacturer of goods to be sold to the uncritical masses. Therefore, all selling of pictures should be stopped. Paintings are not for sale. An artist should not have to try to sell his picture once it has been painted. If the sale of art were prohibited art itself would benefit. The unhealthy speculation in names would disappear and many imitators with it. If society arranged to take over all artistic production and gave the artists what they needed to live, the correct relationship between society and its artists would be established.

Public art libraries should be established over the whole country where people could come and borrow art to take home, just as they do now with books. In certain places this should be done in connection with constantly changing exhibitions. Such an arrangement would be the beginning of a wholly correct solution of the problem. The use of artistic language as a means of communication would be of the greatest significance to our society.

HELHESTEN, Copenhagen, no. 4, n.d. [c. 1943], pp. 92-93

THE STRANGE NIGHT

I am otherwise your lover.
Tonight I returned
To the green duck's house,
I tickled her with
My pointed beard
So strangely
That you refused
To face what was happening
On the meadow.

I am otherwise your hope
That you laid outside
And which shines with a strange
Light
That we gather on
The meadow
To have of this rare silver
The day we will sink
Into hard times.

I am otherwise your deed.
Of all those nights
That we poured
Into bottles
For a hundred years

Till the time
You'll find yourself
And discover with wonder
Your luck spread outside,
Gleaming and nostalgic.
It calls you,
It begs you to swear
That you will remain.

COBRA, Brussels, no. 1, n.d. [1949], p. 7

Alechinsky, *Study in the Morphology of Orange Peels*, 1962

Alechinsky, *Study in the Morphology of Orange Peels*, 1962

CORNEILLE

Come back to your home sweet joy snowing on the pavements
of Paris, gather the golden cocks glittering under your steps;
come forward, come forward still, you shall be pursued for the
rape of a black coffee cup. Shady fellow offspring of my pen
drive back your face of roses and engrave it on the seat of royal
couches, if ever the Squire's groom comes to see, you shall find
yourself of glass and soft young maid.

Pull the mansion's teeth one by one and the sun will enter like
gooseberry juice on the yellow table.

Roll and turn your eyes far from the dreams and the mysteries of
your life of fly, of larva, of telephone number.

Let the Purple Paradises flood the rows of white April flowers,
of blue kisses, of flowery paper cheeks.

Museum-frog, cardboard-cannon, petroleum-tongue, water-belly
brake my morning joy of piano-fish.

Military base, where too many young skirts arrive. Like in but-
terfly days the windowpanes compose words of silk.

Giant trees with green beards, your fruits are enormous cats who
describe the sad moonless nights.

COBRA, Brussels, no. 4, n.d., p. 3

LUCEBERT

ARP

Against the rock's pulse
The hand's thought knocks
The sidewalk's hem rustles
Rocks breath above me
The sea's oxide remains
On the burning-fragile eyes of the earth

Across my mouth there
Breaks the crude slot of the gesture
And my voice signals
Silence, do gallop
No more gravity that thinks

So
Am I betrothed up to my ears with light
Light buys me
It runs over my steps my neck my hair
A human march
The true man who wishes

Silence, do gallop
Through the now still gallopade

GEH DURCH DEN SPIEGEL, Cologne, Galerie Der Spiegel, 1960

Alechinsky, *Study in the Morphology of Orange Peels*, 1962

ASGER JORN

CONCERNING THE ACTUAL VALUE OF THE FUNCTIONALIST CONCEPT

Recent years have brought a growing discontent with rationalist and functionalist concepts. More and more we hear talk of a revolution against their insupportable constraints, and this revolution appears clear and inevitable. But before throwing everything out as waste matter, it is perhaps well to reflect on the character of a real revolution, because a real revolution cannot take place merely by destroying everything.

We should preserve that which appears to be active material in the heritage of functionalism. When the break with the old classicism came, they said "the house is a machine for living", "the kitchen is a machine for eating", etc. These arguments triumphed because of their absolute truth.

The functionalists created a rational analysis of structure and function; they reduced form to its most economical aspect for the satisfaction of our needs. For this reason they created a comprehension of the object and the instrument entirely unknown until then. In addition to this objective functionalism, they attempted a humanistic analysis of the social functions and ethics of our environment, resulting in a democratic base, maintained by an "urban concept", which insists upon the right of man to a habitation which assures him a healthful and calm existence.

In preparing for an irrational architecture, it would be inconceivable to abandon these very important ideas. It is easy, and certainly amusing, to create new concepts opposed to earlier ones, but culture is the opposite of this. Culture is the elaboration and continuous transformation of already existing phenomena. The functionalist slogan can always be useful to us. Utility and function will always remain the point of departure for all formal criticism. It is simply a question of transforming the program of functionalism. It is always valuable to try to reach the greatest result through the most economical means. But if we agree on this point, why are we dissatisfied with functionalism? It is because of its aesthetic, which has never been able to see its aesthetic side as an autonomous function of human activity. Aesthetics is "the science of beauty and ugliness". The functionalists have reached a point where they even deny the autonomous existence of beauty on a Platonic basis, saying "that which is true is good and always beautiful", that is, that logic and ethics contain beauty in themselves.

Because of this false conception they have constructed an aesthetic idea which consists of making the exterior of an object a reflection of the practical functions of its interior and its constructive idea. However, these analyses of utility and necessity, which, according to their ideas, ought to be the basis of the construction of every object made by man, become ridiculous immediately if we profoundly analyze all objects actually manufactured. A fork or a bed cannot possibly be considered absolute necessities for the life and health of man, yet retain, nevertheless, a relative value. In this case, it is a question of "imposed necessity". Modern man is suffocating in necessities like television and frigidaires. He has rendered himself incapable of living his true life. Of course, we are not opposed to modern technology, but we oppose every idea of the absolute necessity of these objects, at times reaching a point where we doubt their effective usefulness.

The functionalists also ignore the psychological function of environment. Thus, the café has no value at all when considered in terms of the health of man, but it has a psychological and sensual importance. Thus, the external appearance of buildings and objects which stand about us have a function independent of their practical use. The exterior of a house should not reflect the interior but should be a source of poetic sensation for those who observe it.

POUR LA FORME, Paris,
L'Internationale Situationniste, 1958, pp. 10-11

CRITIQUE OF THE ORGANIC DOCTRINE OF ARCHITECTURE

Every human technique is inspired by the needs and desires of man. They are the immediate expression of human interest. Hence, the objective and disinterested method of science cannot create any architectural technique.

We must understand that human techniques are purely subjective. Objectively, a house is nothing but a mass of bricks, and a machine no more than an assemblage of iron.

It is man and man alone who can give these things life; no machine moves without the intervention of man, and for the same reason ceases to exist if man no longer interests himself in it.

Naturalist researches into architecture are based on the idea of an organic style, on the model of a tree which grows and develops, for example. This is a valuable concept only if one keeps in mind the fact that man will never know how to make new tires grow on his automobiles when the old ones wear out.

The internal workings of nature are not only different from human techniques; they are workings which unfold according to absolutely opposite laws, according to a fundamentally different law. Nature creates itself from within, evolving from a microscopic cell to a large organism: she grows, so to speak, in opposition to external forces, which makes it impossible for these forms to exist separate from nature. Man can create an absolutely perfect sphere, or a straight line, but nature cannot. This capacity to create independent objects is considered by certain architects, like Corbusier, to be a sign of the superiority of man over nature. But it is not superiority. What makes the sphere of an orange imperfect is the stalk which renders the fruit capable of developing itself, and the seeds which link it to the future. Man is capable of the contrary—he can link and unite two independent objects: a stone with a hole in it and a stick of wood permitted him to construct the first hammer. Man can, moreover, destroy this construction, and he can destroy it at any moment. He can unite a wheel and an axe. Here is the secret of human technique: the ability to unite two apparently independent objects. For those who understand the contradiction of the conception of these two forms of construction (man-nature) nature is a vast field of apprenticeship. We should not forget that man himself is a part of biological life and that, consequently, he has more in common with plants or animals than he does with crystals, the source of inspiration for certain so-called objective architects. Man is a species of organic nature, but one must not forget that all his techniques and his art represent a counter-biological effect in the current of nature, formed by his imagination, his intelligence and his creative power. Actually, all that is anti-natural is destined to be destroyed; that is, man cannot conserve his creations unless they adapt themselves to nature. But he does not have the right, for this reason, to imagine that the evolution of techniques can be put on an empirical basis.

POUR LA FORME, Paris,
L'Internationale Situationniste, 1958, pp. 11-12

BANALITIES

Taste is hereditary—the hyena lives shabbily—Johannes Holbech

It is typical that one who has lost touch with what is fundamental in art also lacks an appreciation of banalities. By this I do not mean the ability to see if something is trite. On the contrary, this ability is developed to a morbid extent. But I do mean the ability to understand the artistic value of banalities, and even their fundamental significance for art itself. There are many anonymous banalities of topical interest that have been passed on through the centuries which far surpass any achievement of genius by our so-called great personalities. If one looks more closely one will also notice that their merit lies in their ability to seize at these banalities.

The great work of art is the complete banality, and the greatest deficiency in most banalities is that they are not trite enough. In this case the banality is not infinite in its depth and consequence, but rests on an inanimate spiritual and aesthetic foundation.

Emancipated banalities have been called natural; they are generalities or truisms, and no attempt has been made to apply the stamp of rarity to them. We must realize that eternal generalities form the very foundation of art; the cheap and inferior are our most precious and indispensable possession.

Nowhere else in the world can one find so many tasteless things as in Paris. This is precisely why Paris is still the place where artistic inspiration lives on.

There is also, for example, a direct strength in the words

Say it
with flowers

which makes this phrase so recurrent in Danish lyricism. It is as worn as an old well-fitting boot and musically can only be compared to those amateur orchestras that play out of tune.

To be able to play out of tune is one of the greatest musical achievements of the day. The search for musical innovation must start with barrel-organs and cheap gramophones.

The greatest musical thrill I have ever experienced took place in a little provincial town where the whole population was seized by an overwhelming desire to play on small magic flutes of celluloid. They were bewitched by this little instrument with its frail piercing warbles, and everywhere in the town, night and day, they played up and down the scale. Every boy and girl, every man and wife, even elderly respectable citizens, went around in secret with the little panpipe in their pockets, and took it out when they thought they were unnoticed in order to imbibe a few warbles from this captivating wonder. Those persons, whose own inner strings were already broken, suffered from this noise which they found irrelevant and annoying. In vain they wrote to the newspapers and made speeches complaining about what they called the "racket".

It was only when influential citizens managed to persuade the police to take action against the trouble-makers, ban the sale of the flutes and arrest all who were in possession of the notorious instruments, that great fear slowly seized the population of the small town so that life could once again return to normal and the depressions so essential to their peace of mind and simple way of life.

I can name many witnesses who can attest to the veracity of this, whereas, as far as I know, no investigations have ever been made into the reasons for those events.

Jens August Schade seems to me to be the only Danish poet who really feels the primary values people create and use in banalities, the only one who consistently builds up his art from this vital material, thus releasing it to such an extent that his poetry grows and renews itself from within the more it is used; just as the fairy tales of Hans Christian Andersen do.

Those who try to fight the production of shoddy pictures are the enemies of the best art in existence today. Those forest lakes in thousands of living rooms covered with golden brown wall-paper are among the deepest sources of artistic inspiration. It is always tragic to see people attempting to saw off the branch on which they are sitting.

The children who love colorful picture postcards and paste them into books with the word "album" printed in front give artists greater hope than art critics and museum directors. Many educators are said to complain that children around the age of twelve stop making good drawings, but they should be happy about this development which is a prerequisite for the human perception of life. I would rather point to the commonplace things that nourish art. The cheap things are the things from "the land below" as described by Gustaf Munch-Petersen. I would like to reproduce this poem in its entirety:

o great joy/they have found great joy/who are born in the land below—/you can see them everywhere/ wandering/loving/crying—/they go everywhere,/but in their hands they carry small things/from the land below—

o greater than all/and more wonderful/is the land below—/the world writhes upwards/into a point—/ and downwards / outwards sinks the heavy / living blood/into the land below—

narrow careful feet/and thin limbs/and clean is the air/over the open rising roads—/in their closed arteries/longing burns in those/who are born up under the heavens—

but oh/you should go to the land below—!/oh, you should see the people from the land below—

where the blood runs freely among all—/men—/ women— / children—/ where joy and despair and love/heavy and full-ripe/shine in all colors unto earth—/oh the earth is as secretive as a brow/in the land below—

everywhere can you see them/wandering/loving/ crying—/their faces are closed,/and on the inside of their souls clings earth/from the land below

In seeking to understand the position of art today, it is also necessary to understand the background for the conditions that have created the development of our artistic perception and our acknowledgment of the relationship between the single individual and society. The artist plays an active part in deepening our knowledge concerning our *raison d'être*, the existence of which makes his artistic creativity possible. An artist's interest cannot be narrowed down to a single field, he must seek the highest perception of the totality and all its details. To him nothing is sacred, because everything has attained meaning.

Selectivity of any kind is out of the question, as it is imperative to penetrate the whole cosmic law of rhythm, power and matter, which is the true world; from the ugliest to the most beautiful, everything that has character and expression; from the most coarse and brutal to the most delicate and gentle, everything which speaks to us by virtue of life.

It follows from this that one must know all in order to be able to express all.

This is the revocation of the aesthetic principle. We are not disillusioned, because we have no illusions; we have never had any.

What we possess and what gives us strength is our joy in life, our interest in life in all its amoral facets. This is also the foundation for today's art. We do not even know the aesthetic laws. The old idea that a choice must be made according to the aesthetic principle, beautiful—ugly, and the ethical, noble—sinful,

is dead to us, for whom the beautiful is also ugly and the ugly endowed with beauty.

Behind the comedy and the tragedy we only find the drama of life, which joins both together, not as noble heroes and false villains, but as human beings.

We know that the man who reads about criminals is reading about something within himself. Beautiful dances and movements do not exist, only expression exists. That which is called beautiful is only an expression for *something*. Our music is not unaesthetic, it has nothing to do with the concept of aesthetics. We refuse to acknowledge the existence of architecture. Only houses and sculpture exist. Housing machines and plastic gigantics. The Cathedral in Cologne is an empty magic piece of sculpture with a purely psychological purpose. A beer glass is architecture.

Style does not exist, and has never existed. Style is the expression of conventional content and form and its varying nuances are called taste.

Absolute separation between painting and sculpture does not exist. Artistic expression cannot be isolated because of its form, it is only various means that are used to attain a common artistic objective. Sandpaper and cotton are just as noble and useful means of expression as oils and marble. These are the guide-lines for the showdown with the conventional concept of art.

The reckoning with idealism as life-philosophy is quite common, but this also touches on something of prime importance in art—its spiritual resources.

It must be understood that it is impossible to differentiate between the form and content of a painting. Just as the structure of a flower is determined by its internal tension (when it loses its sap, it also loses its shape), so it is the content in art that creates the tension. Form and substance are the same. Form is the pattern of life and substance the living painting.

The content of the painting reflects the inner life of the artist and shows to what extent he has sensed himself and his times, how much he embraces and how deep his experiences are rooted.

We cannot expect to inherit a firm, inflexible artistic and philosophic vision from the older generation. Artistic expression varies from period to period, just as our experiences vary. A new experience creates a new form.

We would like to learn everything we need from earlier generations, but we ourselves must find out *what* it is that we need because nobody else can do it for us. It is not our duty to receive and work with what the older generation would like us to do. On the contrary, it is their duty to help us, when and where we want their help.

The explanation that I have attempted to set forth here deals with questions of such an intimate nature that every human being is involved. Nobody can withdraw his personality from this point. *The spectator can no longer exist in our times.*

HELHESTEN, Copenhagen, vol. 1, no. 2, n.d. [c. 1942], pp. 33-39

RENÉ MAGRITTE

Inspired thought—of which the pictorial description is possible—resembles only those forms presented by the world *through that which is visible*. My painting *The Waterfall* is the description of an inspired thought which can be found simultaneously in the forest and away from the forest. In fact, this thought unites the foliage that is inside the forest with a painting which allows a distant forest to appear.

I identify the description of such a thought with poetry.

The title *The Waterfall* suggests that this inspired thought gushed forth like a waterfall.

1963

Magritte, *Sketches for "The Waterfall"*. Collection Mr. and Mrs. Harry Torczyner, New York.

THOUGHT AND IMAGES

It is possible to be "struck" by the word Thought. Our thought is concerned with diverse sensations, feelings, reflexes, preferences, activities, ideas, beliefs and preoccupations, as if the thought which "coincides" with these "things" was the only possible thought, as if the thought which coincides still deserved the name of thought.

—"What difference!" some will say. —"It's the pleasure of an agreeable and strong sensation that counts!" Or: —"It's fulfilling my obligation!" But, undoubtedly, in order that it "count", thought is necessary, which "praises" the pleasure or the obligation.

The hand which comes too close to the fire and the reflex action which causes a scream of pain and causes the hand to be drawn away from the flames "count", at the same moment, for thought, which is obliged to concern itself with a painful sensation and a reflex action. It *coincides* exactly, at that instant, with those two things. The *coincidence* is no less exact when, at other moments, the mind takes "count" of the advisability and the misgivings which it is considering. The *coincidence* remains the same so long as it is a question of the complexity of a simultaneous attention to a greater number of things: at the same time for the exquisite savoring of a soup, for the beauty of the hostess, and for an idea on the origin of thought or for a professional problem.

*　*　*

To think an image means to See an image.

The painting introduces a palpable image into sight. The sight registers without Seeing, in reverse, according to optic laws and like a camera, the image presented by the painting. In the mind this image becomes a moral image, that is to say an image having a spiritual value. It is thought which gives this value.

*　*　*

The images which paintings offer may be endowed with improper values: commercial "value", for example; or the one prized by those maniacs concerned above all with the metrical dimensions of the painting, by the resolute partisans of small or large portions of space, by the champions for the proper sizing of frescoes, the arrangement of supports, the authenticity of cracks and the composition of pastes and recanvassing, by the experts in matters of anatomy, perspective or projected shadows.

The values which truly relate to the image are dependent, according to personal preferences, upon one or several aesthetic theories which condition the making of paintings or which result from them. The fear of being mystified surely relates also to the painted image which has the force to provoke such a fear.

A "very safe" choice can easily be made between the glory of the impressionists, the dynamism of the futurists, the cubism of Picasso, the abstract art of Mondrian or Archipenko and the genius of de Chirico. It is equally possible to give value to the latest well-schooled *Prix de Rome* or even to "vibrate" with the "young" (and the old) who bewilder art criticism with their 1954 "discovery" of abstraction and nonfiguration.

*　*　*

Men, women and children who never think about the history of art have personal preferences, just as much as the aesthetes. The discordancy of preferences cannot be explained by the influences of different *milieus*. In fact, "Siamese twins" generally have dissimilar tastes and opposing beliefs no more or less than one individual who is twofold, notably by his conflicting desires. If

sentimental differences are "explained" by determining differences in the conformation of "gray matter", it is obvious that this "explanation" is not enlightening and that it very much resembles the responses administered by the doctors of Molière.

It is thought which permits an "explanation." It is thought which awards value. Whether the explanation be of a theological, metaphysical, psychological or biological order, it is "issued" by the mind, which explains *without ever explaining itself*, whatever may seem to be.

Our life, deprived of thought, could doubtlessly endure, like that of a plant, of which it is not known if it "thinks." It is thought which awards a value to life. All values are the gifts of the mind. That which gives is free. The mind is essentially free. It is the Light. However, in the ordinary and extraordinary moments of life, our mind does not manifest all its freedom. It is unceasingly menaced, engaged by everything that happens to us. It *coincides* with a thousand and one things that limit it. This coincidence is *almost* permanent.

The mind has a certain freedom when, for example, it awards value to the sympathy one feels for a stone or when it accords the greatest value to life and to the Universe, on which life depends. One should, for his freedom, love Ruskin, that art lover, when he writes: "Let all the works of art perish sooner than the birds which sing in the trees."

Life, the Universe, Nothingness have no value for the mind in the plenitude of its liberty. For it, the only Value is Meaning, that is to say the moral thought of the Impossible. To think the Meaning signifies for the mind to free itself of ideas which are ordinary, almost ordinary or extraordinary.

*　*　*

In the realm of the arts, thought is generally deprived of all freedom by respect for dead traditions or by obedience to ridiculous fashions.

*　*　*

The absurdity and the ill-nature of the world entreat the revolt of the generous heart and the attention of the mind for justice.

*　*　*

My paintings are images. The valid description of an image cannot be made without the orientation of the mind toward its freedom. One must be at once attentive to the image and to the words which are chosen to describe it. The description of the painted image turned into spiritual image in the mind, must be *indefinitely perfectible*. It is of importance, moreover, to be suspicious of the inopportune usage of certain words (abstract, concrete, consciousness, unconsciousness, imaginary, real, mystification, sincerity, reason, madness, palette, literature, temperament, ideal, etc.).

I consider as valid the attempt of language which consists in saying that my paintings were conceived in order to be material signs of the freedom of thought. They aspire, within all the "bounds of the possible", not to be unworthy of Meaning, that is to say the Impossible.

To be able to answer the question: "What is the *meaning* of these images?", would correspond to making Meaning, the Impossible, resemble a possible idea. To attempt to answer would be acknowledging a *meaning* to it. The spectator is able to see, with the greatest possible freedom my images *such as they are*, while trying like their author to think of the Meaning, which is to say the Impossible.

Palais des Beaux-Arts, Brussels, 1954, MAGRITTE.

BIBLIOGRAPHY

The bibliography is arranged in three stages of decreasing generality: first art on an international scale; next national groups; then individual artists. The choice of entries has been rigorously selective; where existing recent bibliographies are easily available reference is made to them, and the contents not repeated.

INTERNATIONAL ART

Recurring Exhibitions

XXIX BIENNALE INTERNAZIONALE D'ARTE, Venice, 1958. Introduction by Gian Alberto Dell'Acqua.

> *Quadrum*, Brussels, no. 6, 1959. Giuseppe Marchiori, "La XXIX Biennale di Venezia", pp. 45–50; Herta Wescher, "Les Participations Espagnole et Yugoslave à la XXIXe Biennale de Venise", pp. 51–68; James Fitzsimmons, "Space and the Image in Art (à propos of the Biennale of Venice)", pp. 69–86.

> RUSSELL, JOHN. "Summer Roundup: Venice Biennale", *Art in America*, New York, vol. 46, no. 2, Summer, 1958, pp. 85, 86.

XXX BIENNALE INTERNAZIONALE D'ARTE, Venice, 1960. Introduction by Gian Alberto Dell'Acqua.

> *Art International*, Zürich, vol. 4, no. 7, September 25, 1960. Lawrence Alloway, "Venice-Europe 1960", pp. 26–29; Friedrich Bayl, "Von ironischen und tragischen Pathos der XXX Biennale", pp. 33–35; Maurizio Calvesi, "La Scultura italiana alla XXX Biennale", pp. 73, 77.

> *Aujourd'hui*, Paris, vol. 5, no. 27, June, 1960. J.-A. Franca, "XXXe Biennale de Venise", pp. 54–55; Denys Chevalier, "XXXeme Biennale de Venise", pp. 56–57.

> HABASQUE, GUY. "La XXXe Biennale de Venise", *L'Oeil*, Paris, no. 69, September, 1960, pp. 26–35, 54.

> KELLER, HEINZ. "XXX Biennale internazionale d'Arte", *Werk*, Winterthur, no. 47, August, 1960, pp. 161–165.

> TILLIM, SIDNEY. "Report on the Venice Biennale", *Arts*, New York, vol. 35, no. 1, October, 1960, pp. 28–35.

XXXI BIENNALE INTERNAZIONALE D'ARTE, Venice, 1962. Introduction by Gian Alberto Dell'Acqua.

> *Art International*, Zürich, vol. 6, no. 8, October 25, 1962. Lawrence Alloway, "Venezorama", pp. 33–36; Gualtiero Schöenberger, "Alla XXXI Biennale di Venezia", pp. 36–38; Françoise Choay, "Venise 1962", pp. 38–40.

> HABASQUE, GUY. "La XXXIe Biennale", *L'Oeil*, Paris, no. 93, September, 1962, pp. 32–41, 72–73.

> KELLER, HEINZ. "Venedig: XXXI Biennale", *Werk*, Winterthur, vol. 49, August, 1962, pp. 183–187.

> MICHELSON, ANNETTE. "Venice Biennale", *Arts*, New York, vol. 37, no. 1, October, 1962, pp. 20–26.

> RESTANY, PIERRE. "La Biennale de Venise à 67 ans", *Ring des Arts*, Zürich, no. 3, December 1962, pp. 7–13.

II DOCUMENTA, KUNST NACH 1945, INTERNATIONALE AUSTELLUNG, Kassel, vol. 1, *Malerei*, introduction by Werner Haftmann; vol. 2, *Skulptur*, introduction by Eduard Trier; vol. 3, *Druckgrafik*, introduction by Albrecht Fabri.

> *Art International*, Zürich, vol. 3, no. 7, 1959. Lawrence Alloway, "Before and After 1945: Reflections on Documenta

II", pp. 29–36, 79; Friedrich Bayl, "Die II Documenta", pp. 37–42; Pierre Restany, "Documenta II: le plus colossal des témoinages du Présent", pp. 43–56.

HAFTMANN, WERNER. "On the Content of Contemporary Art", *Quadrum*, Brussels, no. 7, 1959, pp. 5–22. (Lecture given at Documenta II inauguration.)

KELLER, HEINZ. "II Documenta '59 museum Fridericianum", *Werk*, Winterthur, vol. 46, Summer, 1959, pp. 196–197.

THWAITES, JOHN ANTHONY. "Report on Documenta II", *Arts*, New York, vol. 34, no. 2, November, 1959, pp. 44–49.

DEPARTMENT OF FINE ARTS, CARNEGIE INSTITUTE, Pittsburgh, December 5, 1958–February 8, 1959. *1958, Pittsburgh Bicentennial International Exhibition Of Contemporary Painting and Sculpture.*

DEPARTMENT OF FINE ARTS, CARNEGIE INSTITUTE, Pittsburgh, December 5, 1958–February 8, 1959. *Retrospective Exhibition of Previous Internationals 1896–1955.* Text by Anthony Arkus.

DEPARTMENT OF FINE ARTS, CARNEGIE INSTITUTE, Pittsburgh, October 27, 1961–January 7, 1962. *1961, Pittsburgh International Exhibition of Contemporary Painting and Sculpture.*

RUBIN, WILLIAM. "The International Style: Notes on the Pittsburgh Triennial", *Art International*, Zürich, vol. 5, no. 9, 1961, pp. 26–34.

WORLD'S FAIR, Seattle, April 21–October 21, 1962, *Art Since 1950.* Introductions by Sam Hunter and Willem Sandberg.

LANGSNER, JULES. "Clues to the Art of Our Time: the exhibitions at the Seattle World's Fair", *Art International*, Zürich, vol. 6, no. 4, May, 1962, pp. 31–46.

PALAZZO GRASSI, CENTRO INTERNAZIONALE DELLE ARTI E DEL COSTUME, Venice, August–October, 1959, *Vitalita Nell'Arte.* Texts by Paolo Marinotti, Henry Michaux, Willem Sandberg.

PALAZZO GRASSI, CENTRO INTERNAZIONALE DELLE ARTI E DEL COSTUME, Venice, July 7–October 2, 1960, *Della Natura All'Arte.* Text by Paolo Marinotti.

PALAZZO GRASSI, CENTRO INTERNAZIONALE DELLE ARTI E DEL COSTUME, Venice, July–October, 1961, *Arte e Contemplazione.* Texts by Paolo Marinotti, Willem Sandberg.

PALAZZO GRASSI, CENTRO INTERNAZIONALE DELLE ARTI E DEL COSTUME, Venice, July–October, 1963, *Vision e Colore.* Texts by Paolo Marinotti, Christian Dotremont.

Single Exhibitions

KUNSTHALLE, Bern, January 29–March 6, 1955, *Tendances Actuelles.* Foreword by Arnold Rüdlinger and Michel Tapié.

INSTITUTE OF ARTS, Minneapolis, September 23–Actober 25, 1959, *European Art Today.* Edited with an introduction by Sam Hunter. Articles by Lawrence Alloway, Umbro Apollonio, Friedrich Bayl, J. E. Cirlot, James Fitzsimmons.

STADTISCHES MUSEUM, Leverkusen, March 15–May 8, 1960, *Monochrome Malerei.* Including texts by Enrico Castellani, Otto Peine, Arnulf Rainer and others.

HAUS AM WALDSEE, Berlin-Zehlendorf, September 25–November 20, 1962, *Sculpturale Malerei.* Texts by Manfred de la Motte and others.

STAATISCHE KUNSTHALLE, Baden-Baden, *Mostra di Pittura Contemporanea Comunitá Europa, 1962–1963, Premio Marsotto.* Text by C. A. B. Morucchio, Roland Penrose, Herbert Read, and Michel Tapié.

STEDELIJK MUSEUM, Amsterdam, May 3–June 10, 1963, *Schrift en Beeld.* Texts by Franz Morr and others.

MUSÉE CANTONAL DES BEAUX-ARTS, Lausanne, June–September, 1963, *1e Salon International de Galeries Pilotes.* Text by Raymonde Moulin. [An exhibition of artists grouped by galleries]

Books

BRION, MARCEL AND OTHERS. *Art Since 1945*, New York, Abrams, n.d. [1958]

BAYL, FRIEDRICH. *Bilder unserer Tage*, Cologne, Dumont Schauberg, 1960.

PONENTE, NELLO. *Contemporary Trends*, Geneva, Skira, 1960.

RESTANY, PIERRE. *Lyrisme et Abstraction*, Milan, Edizione Apollinaire, 1960.

BAYER, RAYMOND. *L'Esthétique mondiale au Vingtième Siècle*, Paris, Presses Universitaire de France, 1961.

MATHIEU, GEORGES. *Au-Dela du Tachisme*, Paris, Julliard, 1963. [Including reprints of documents of late 1940's and early 50's]

SEUPHOR, MICHEL. *Abstract Painting*, New York, Abrams, n.d. [See Part III: "After 1940"]

Magazines

HUNTER, SAM. "Painting by Another Name", *Art in America*, New York, vol. 42, no. 4, December, 1954, pp. 291–295.

MATHIEU, GEORGES AND OTHERS. "Les Documents de la Révolution", *La Tour de Feu*, Paris, no. 51, Autumn, 1956, pp. 71–96. [Collection of texts 1946–1955, dealing with post war abstract painting in Paris, reprinted mainly from catalogues]

XXe Siècle, Paris, vol. 20, no. 10, March, 1958 [Issue devoted to "L'Ecriture Plastique"]

TILLIM, SIDNEY. "What Happened to Geometry?", *Arts*, New York, vol. 33, no. 9, June, 1959, pp. 38–44. [Reprinted in *The Best in Arts*, (Arts Yearbook 6) New York, Arts Magazine, n.d. [1962], pp. 106–111.]

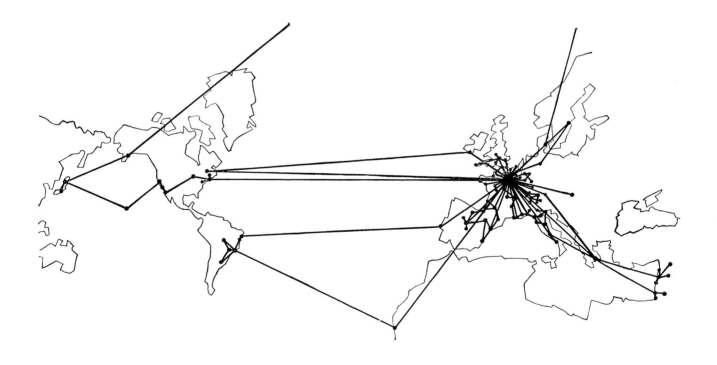

"Principal Travels of Georges Mathieu"

I.

MALRAUX, ANDRÉ. *The Voices of Silence*, Garden City, Doubleday, 1953. [See section "Museum without Walls", pp. 13–131 for the relation of original works to art reproductions.]

GOMBRICH, E. H. "André Malraux and the Crisis of Expressionism", *Burlington Magazine*, London, vol. 96, no. 621, December, 1954, pp. 374–378.

HAUSER, ARNOLD. *The Philosophy of Art History*, London, Routledge and Kegan Paul, 1959. [See pp. 241–247 on Malraux.]

BOORSTIN, DANIEL. J. *The Image*, New York, Atheneum, 1962. [See "From Traveller to Tourist: The Lost Art of Travel" and "From Shapes to Shadows: Dissolving Forms", pp. 77–180. 'Almost without exception, whatever one sees in a museum is seen out of its proper surroundings. The impression of individual works of art or of the country's past culture as a whole . . . is inevitably factitious', p. 101. As a result of reproduction processes 'the original itself acquires a technical esoteric status', 'a prototype . . . from which other mass-produced items are made', p. 127.]

FRANK, JOSEPH. "Malraux's Metaphysics of Art", *The Sewanee Review*, Sewanee, Tennessee, vol. 70, no. 4, 1962, pp. 620–650.

WIND, EDGAR. *Art and Anarchy*, Faber and Faber, London, 1963. [See section "The Mechanization of Art" for the argument that 'the medium of diffusion tends to take over the direct experience of the object']

RESTANY, PIERRE. "Panorama Internationale de la critique d'art contemporaine", *Domus*, Milan, no. 401, April 4, 1963, pp. 28–32.

II. OLD WORLD, NEW WORLD

KOUWENHOVEN, JOHN A. *Made in America, the Artist in Modern Civilization*, Garden City, Doubleday, 1948. [At attempt to define distinctive American characteristics in culture] Revised edition published by Anchor, 1962.

HESS, THOMAS B. "The Cigarbox of Napoleon III: Some notes on the battle between French Art and Paris Art", *Yale French Studies*, New Haven, nos. 19–20, 1957, pp. 45–49.

ROSENBERG, HAROLD. *The Tradition of the New*, New York, Horizon Press, 1959. [See chapters 1, 2, 7, 15; pp. 13–39, 87–95, 209–220; Americans as coonskinners, Europeans as redcoats]

GREENBERG, CLEMENT. *Art and Culture*, Boston, Beacon Press, 1961. [See "School of Paris: 1946", pp. 120–133; "Contribution to a Symposium", pp. 124–126; "American Type Painting", pp. 208–229]

BOORSTIN, DANIEL J. *America and the Image of Europe: Reflections on American Thought*, New York, Meridian, 1960. [See "American Style–Historical Monuments", pp. 81–86]

ASHTON, DORE. *The Unknown Shore: a view of contemporary art*, Boston, Atlantic-Little Brown, 1962. [See part 1, pp. 3–128, on "The American Note" and part II "European Counterpoint", pp. 131–170]

MC COUBREY, JOHN W. *American Tradition in Painting*, New York, Braziller, 1963. [An attempt to define the 'inherent expressiveness' of American paintings]

ROSENBERG, HAROLD. "The Art Galleries: 'On Art Movements'",

The New Yorker, New York, October 5, 1963, pp. 159–162, 164, 167–169. [Partly a review of McCoubrey]

MATHIEU, GEORGES. *Au-Dela du Tachisme*, Paris, Julliard, 1963. [See "Diffusion et Contagion Mondiales 1956–1962", pp. 115–151]

III. COBRA

[An attempt to define a North European Style. Name formed from COpenhagen, BRussels, Amsterdam.]

Helhesten, Copenhagen, 5 issues, 1941–43.

Reflex, Organn van de experimentale groep in Holland, 2 issues, 1948.

Cobra, Brussels, Bulletin pour la coordination des investigations artistiques lien souple des groupes experimentaux Danois (Høst) ; Belge (Surréaliste-Revolutionaire) ; Hollandais (Reflex), 10 numbers, 1948–1951.

STEDELIJK MUSEUM, Amsterdam, May 10–June 10, 1957, *Phases*. Texts by Edouard Jaguer, Pierre Alechinsky, etc.

GALERIE K.-K., Copenhagen, September 30–October 14, 1961, *Cobra*. Text by Troels Andersen.

ANDERSEN, TROELS. "The 'Linien' group of painters", *Signum*, Gyldendal, vol. 1, no. 2, 1961, pp. 10–31. [English summary, p. 63]

STATENS MUSEUM FUR KUNST, Copenhagen, 1961, *Fru Elise Johansens Samling*.

RAGON, MICHEL. "La groupe Cobra et l'Expressionisme Lyrique", *Cimaise*, Paris, vol. 9, no. 59, May–June, 1962, pp. 26–45. [Text also in English, Spanish, German]

ALLOWAY, LAWRENCE. "Danish Art and Primitivism", *Living Arts*, London, no. 1, 1963, pp. 44–52.

IV. EAST-WEST

DUTHUIT, GEORGES. *Chinese Mysticism and Modern Painting*, Paris, Chronique des Jours; London, Zwemmer, 1936.

MAC AGY, DOUGLAS, ed. "The Western Round Table on Modern Art [1949]", *Modern Artists in America* [first series], New York, Wittenborn, Schultz, n.d. [1951]. [See "The Cultural Setting: Intelligibility and Communications", pp. 27–28]

ALECHINSKY, PIERRE. "Calligraphie Japonais", *Quadrum*, Brussels, no. 1, 1956, pp. 43–52.

ALECHINSKY, PIERRE. "De Japanse Calligraphie; Een Nieuwe Phase", *Museumjournal*, Eindhoven, series 2, no. 1–2, September, 1956, pp. 1–5.

ALECHINSKY, PIERRE. "Japanese Calligraphy and Abstraction", *Graphis*, Zürich, vol. 12, no. 68, 1956, pp. 542–553.

VON WIEGAND, C. "The Oriental Tradition and its Environment", *The World of Abstract Art*, New York, Wittenborn, 1957, pp. 55–68.

"Eastern Artists Western Artists", *International Association of Plastic Arts Information Bulletin*, Paris, February, 1961. Special issue devoted to meeting in Vienna, September, 1960. Speeches by Mark Tobey and others.

NATIONAL STYLES

The following articles appear in *Encyclopédie de l'art international contemporain*, Paris, Prisme des Arts, 1958:

AUSTRIA: Hofmann, Werner. "L'art contemporain en Autriche", pp. 57–64; BELGIUM: Delevoy, Robert. "L'art contemporain en Belgique", pp. 65–72; DENMARK: Schultz, Sigurd and Schwartz, Walter. "L'art contemporain au Danemark", pp. 101–104; GERMANY: Roh, Franz. "L'art contemporain en Allemagne", pp. 25–32; HUNGARY: Genthon, Etienne. "L'art contemporain en Hongrie, pp. 165–168; ISRAEL: Baram, Sioma. "L'art contemporain en Israël", pp. 177–184; MEXICO: Nelken, Margarita. "L'art contemporain du Mexique", pp. 209–216; THE NETHERLANDS: Braat, L. P. J. "L'art contemporain aux Pays-Bas", pp. 225–232; NORWAY: Revold, Reidar. "L'art contemporain au Norwège", pp. 217–220; POLAND: Starzynski, Juliusz. "L'art contemporain en Pologne", pp. 233–240; SPAIN: Cirlot, Juan-Eduardo and Gudiol, José. "L'art contemporain en Espagne", pp. 105–112; SWEDEN: Lindwall, Bo. "L'art contemporain en Suède", pp. 241–244.

ARGENTINA

VIAU GALERÍA DE ARTE. Buenos Aires, 1952, *Grupo de artistas modernos de la Argentina*. Preface by Aldo Pellegrini.

AUSTRIA

ARTS COUNCIL OF GREAT BRITAIN, London, 1960, *Austrian Painting and Sculpture, 1900–1960*. Introduction by Werner Hofmann. Includes artists' biographies.

BELGIUM

LANGUI, ÉMILE. "L'art contemporain en Belgique", *L'Oeil*, Paris, no. 40, April, 1958, pp. 88–95.

Aujourd'hui: Art et Architecture, Boulogne-sur-Seine, no. 27, June, 1960. Special issue devoted to Belgium. Maurits Bilcke, "Les premiers abstraits en Belgique", p. 4–7; Edouard Jaguer, "Au pays des images défendues", pp. 10–19; Raoul Vaneigem, "Tendances de la nouvelle peinture abstraite en Belgique", pp. 20–27.

PARKE-BERNET GALLERIES, New York. June 29–August 5, 1960, *The Arts of Belgium 1920–1961*. "The Arts" by J. Van Leberghe.

CANADA

CASO, P. "L'art contemporain au Canada", *Canadian Art*, Ottawa, no. 15, August, 1958, pp. 188, 239.

FULFORD, ROBERT. "A Survey of the Work of 24 Young Canadian Artists", *Canadian Art*, Ottawa, vol. 18, no. 1, January, 1961, pp. 8–55.

BAGNANI, GILBERT and others. "A Survey of the Work of 21 More Canadian Artists", *Canadian Art*, Ottawa, vol. 19, no. 2, March–April, 1962, pp. 112–153.

PALAZZO COLLICOLA, Spoleto, 5° Festival dei due Mondi, June 26–August 23, 1962, *La Peinture Canadienne Moderne*.

GREENBERG, CLEMENT. "Painting and Sculpture in Prairie Canada Today", *Canadian Art*, Ottawa, vol. 20, no. 2, March–April, 1963, pp. 90–107. [See also *Canadian Art*, Ottawa, vol. 20, no. 3, 1963, "Letters to the Editor. South of the Borduas–Down 10th Street Way", Moncrieff Williamson, p. 196.]

DENMARK

POULSEN, VAGN. *Danish Painting and Sculpture*, Copenhagen, Danske Selskab, 1955.

YOUNG, VERNON. "Report from Copenhagen", *Arts*, New York, vol. 32, no. 6, March, 1958, pp. 24–28.

COLDING, STEEN. "Present Day Danish Art", *European Art This Month*, Zürich, vol. 1, nos. 9–10, 1958, pp. 31–32, 46–49.

KJAERHOLM, HANS. *Hvorfor Maler de Saadan*, [Why do they paint like that?] Copenhagen, G.E.C. Gads, 1959.

HULTÉN, K. G. "Jeunes peintres danois et suédois", *L'Oeil*, Paris, no. 98, February, 1963, pp. 58–67.

FRANCE

"Symposium: Is the French Avant-Garde Overrated?" *Art Digest*, New York, vol. 27, no. 20, September 15, 1953, pp. 12–13, 27. Discussion by Ralston Crawford, Clement Greenberg, Robert Motherwell, Jack Tworkov.

ALVARD, JULIEN. "Paris sans école", *Cimaise*, Paris, vol. 3, no. 1, October–November, 1955, pp. 10–11.

GINDERTAEL, R. V. "Le complexe de l'École de Paris", *Cimaise*, Paris, vol. 3, no. 4, March, 1956, p. 9.

Arts Yearbook, 3, New York, 1959. "Paris/New York", including "Paris" by André Masson; "New York" by Stuart Davis; "French Art and the Post War Crisis" by M. W. Ray; "Painters of the 1950's".

MORAND, KATHLEEN. "Post-war Trends in École de Paris", *Burlington Magazine*, London, vol. 102, no. 686, May, 1960, pp. 187–192.

GINDERTAEL, R. V. "Reflexions sur l'École de Paris", *Quadrum*, Brussels, no. 9, 1960, pp. 35–48, 192.

GERMANY

HÄNDLER, GERHARD. *German Painting in our Time*, Berlin, Rembrandt-Verlag, 1956.

BAYL, FRIEDRICH. "Keine Experimente", *European Art This Month*, Zürich, vol. 1, nos. 9–10, 1958, pp. 23–24, 32.

THWAITES, JOHN ANTHONY. "New German Painting", *Art in America*, New York, vol. 50, no. 3, Fall, 1962, pp. 118–123.

HUNGARY

MUSÉE RATH, Geneva, 1961, *Art Hongrois; XIXe et XXe Siècles*.

ISRAEL

GAMZU, HAIM. *Painting and Sculpture in Israel*, Tel Aviv, Dvir, 1958. [revised edition]

RIVIÈRE, CLAUDE. "L'art en Israël", *XXe Siècle*, Paris, no. 13, December, 1959. [*Chroniques du Jour*, unpaginated supplement]

FRAMPTON, KENNETH. "Modern Art in Israel", *Art News and Review*, London, vol. 11, no. 11, June 20, 1959, p. 2.

Aujourd'hui: Art et Architecture, Boulogne-sur-Seine, no. 26, April, 1960. Special issue devoted to Israel. Samuel Dubiner, "L'Art Israelien d'aujourd'hui", p. 11; Yona Fischer, "Les arts plastiques en Israel", p. 11–26; "La situation de l'artiste en Israel", p. 27.

JAPAN

MUNSTERBERG, HUGO. "East and West in Contemporary Japanese Art", *College Art Journal*, New York, vol. 18, no. 1, Fall, 1958, pp. 36–41.

ICHINOSE, THOMAS T. "L'art abstrait au Japon", *Art Actuel International*, no. 7, 1959, pp. 4–6.

BECKH, ERICA. "Contemporary Art in Japan", *College Art Journal*, New York, vol. 19, no. 1, Fall, 1959, pp. 10–22.

LATIN AMERICA

Art in America, New York, vol. 47, no. 3, Fall, 1959, pp. 22–47. Special section on Pan American painting. José Gomez Sicre, *Trends Latin American*.

PLATSCHEK, HANS. "Notizen zur malerei Latinamerikas", *Das Kunstwerk*, Baden-Baden, vol. 13, no. 5–6, November, 1959, p. 66.

DE SZYSZLO, FERNANDO. "Contemporary Latin American Painting; a brief survey", *College Art Journal*, New York, no. 2, Winter, 1959–60, pp. 134–145.

MEXICO

FERNANDEZ, JUSTINE. *Arte Moderno y Contemporaneo de Mexico*, Mexico City, Imprinta universitaria, 1952. Introduction by Manuel Toussaint. [bibliography]

ASHTON, DORE. "Art: the Mexican Art World", *Arts and Architecture*, Los Angeles, no. 75, October, 1958, pp. 4, 36, 37.

CARDOZA Y ARAGÓN. *Mexico: Pintura Activa*, Mexico City, Era, 1961.

NELKEN, MARGARITA. "Nuevos aspectos de la plastica mexicana", *Artes de Mexico*, Colonia Santa Maria Insurgentes, vol. 6, no. 33, 1961, pp. 1–14.

NORWAY

ANKER, PETER. "Abstrakt kunst: Norge", *Paletten*, Göteborg, no. 3, 1957, pp. 81–85.

HULTÉN, K. G. "Jeunes peintres danois et suédois", *L'Oeil*, Paris, no. 98, February, 1963, pp. 58–67.

POLAND

WOZNIAKOWSKI, JACEK. "L'art en Pologne et la liquidation du réalisme socialiste", *Prisme des Arts*, Paris, no. 6, November, 1956, p. 41.

JAGUER, EDOUARD. "L'avant-garde Polonaise, structure et dynamique", *Cahiers du Musée de Poche*, Paris, no. 4, May, 1960, pp. 40–54.

RESTANY, PIERRE. "Die Situation der Kunst in Polen", *Das Kunstwerk*, Baden-Baden, vol. 14, no. 8, February, 1961, pp. 16–18.

LANGSNER, JULES. "Modern Art in Poland; the legacy and the revival", *Art International*, Zürich, vol. 5, no. 1, September 20, 1961, pp. 22–29.

JELENSKI, K. A. " 'L'art informel' and non-conformity", *Arts*, New York, vol. 36, no. 2, November, 1961, pp. 52–59.

THE MUSEUM OF MODERN ART, New York, 1961, *15 Polish Painters*. Text by Peter Selz.

SPAIN

POPOVICI, C. "L'art abstrait en Espagne", *Cimaise*, Paris, vol. 3, no. 1, October–November, 1955, pp. 7–9.

CHOAY, FRANÇOISE. "L'école espagnole", *L'Oeil*, Paris, no. 51, March, 1959, pp. 10–17.

ROH, FRANZ. "Junge Spanische Malerei", *Das Kunstwerk*, Baden-Baden, vol. 13, no. 7, January, 1960, pp. 13–21.

THE MUSEUM OF MODERN ART, New York, July 13–September 25, 1960, [circulated in the United States], *New Spanish Painting and Sculpture*. Text by Frank O'Hara.

JELENSKI, K. A. " 'L'art informel' and non-conformity", *Arts*, New York, vol. 36, no. 3, December, 1961, pp. 32–35.

ATENEO DE MADRID, Madrid, 1962, *20 Anos de Pintura Espanola*. Texts by Juan Antonia Gaya Nuño, R. Santos Torroella, José de Castro Arines.

SWEDEN

SÖDERBERG, ROLF. "Abstrait en Suède", *Art d'Aujourd'hui*, Paris, vol. 4, no. 7, October–November, 1953, pp. 1–11.

JOHNSON, ELLEN H. "Decade of Swedish Painting", *Arts*, New York, vol. 36, no. 6, March, 1962, pp. 16–20.

SWITZERLAND

DU, Zürich, vol. 19, no. 222, August, 1959. Special issue devoted to Swiss artists under age 35.

HILTY, HANS RUDOLF, ed. *Die dritte Generation, 42 junge Schweizer Künstler*, St. Gallen, Tschudy, 1960. [Published in connection with exhibition at Kunstmuseum, St. Gallen, May–June, 1960 "42 junge Schweizer"]

UNITED KINGDOM

ALLOWAY, LAWRENCE. "English and International Art", *European Art This Month*, Zürich, vol. 1, nos. 9–10, 1958, pp. 54–55.

Aujourd'hui: Art et Architecture, Boulogne-sur-Seine, no. 25, February, 1960. Charles Delloye, "L'art Anglais d'aujourd'hui; Sioma Baram, "Moyens et buts des arts plastiques en Angleterre", pp. 6–14.

UNITED STATES

Aujourd'hui: Art et Architecture, Boulogne-sur-Seine, vol. 2, no. 6, June, 1951. Special issue "La peinture aux Etats-Unis d'Amérique", J. Alvard, "Quelques jeunes Américains de Paris"; Michel Seuphor, Paris–New York, 1951; George L. K. Morris, Willem de Kooning, Stuart Davis, and others, "La Peinture Abstrait aux U.S.A."

"Symposium: Is the American Avant-garde Overrated?", *Art Digest*, New York, vol. 28, no. 2, October 15, 1953, pp. 10–11, 33, 34. Discussion by Jean Dubuffet, Alfred Manessier, Georges Mathieu.

RESTANY, PIERRE. "L'art aux Etats-Unis: J. Pollock, l'écablousseur", *Prisme des Arts*, Paris, no. 15, 1957.

COURTOIS, MICHEL. "Huits artists réputés d'outre Atlantique montent l'absence de caractère national dans l'art Américain actuel", *Arts*, Paris, March 12, 1958.

CHOAY, FRANÇOISE. "Pseudo-École du Pacifique," *France Observateur*, Paris, May 27, 1958.

RUBIN, WILLIAM. "The New York School Then and Now", *Art International*, Zürich, part 1, vol. 2, nos. 2–3, 1958, pp. 23–26; part 2, vol. 2, nos. 4–5, 1958, pp. 19–22.

Cimaise, Paris, vol. 6, no. 3, January–March, 1959. Special issue "Nouveaux regards sur l'art aux Etats-Unis", includes: Michel Ragon, "L'art actuel aux Etats-Unis"; Pierre Restany, "U.S. Go Home and Come Back Later".

HAMILTON, GEORGE HEARD. "Painting in Contemporary America", *Burlington Magazine*, London, no. 102, May, 1960, pp. 192–197.

"International Look at the U.S.A.", *Art in America*, New York, vol. 48, no. 2, Summer, 1960, pp. 22–65. Articles by Pierre Jeannerat and others.

JACOBS, RACHEL. "L'idéologie de la peinture Américaine", *Aujourd'hui: Art et Architecture*, Boulogne-sur-Seine, vol. 6, no. 27, 1962, pp. 6–19.

VENEZUELA

MUSEO DE BELLAS ARTES, Caracas, April 19–July 5, 1961. *Pintura Venezolana 1661–1961*. Text by Guillermo Menses.

INDIVIDUAL ARTISTS

Statements by artists are given first, followed by critical texts and catalogues arranged chronologically.

PIERRE ALECHINSKY

1927, Brussels. École Nationale Supérieure d'Architecture et des Arts Décoratifs, Brussels, 1944; engraving at Atelier 17, 1952. Founding member of *Cobra* group. First one-man exhibition, Galerie Lou Cosyn, Brussels, 1947. Resident Paris.

Alechinsky, Pierre. "Abstraction Faite", *Cobra 10*, Brussels, 1951, pp. 6–8.

Alechinsky, Pierre. "Calligraphie Japonaise", *Quadrum*, Brussels, no. 1, May, 1956, pp. 43–52.

Alechinsky, Pierre and d'Haese, Reinhoud. "Study in the Morphology of Orange Peels", *Situationist Times*, Hengelo, Holland, no. 3, 1963, pp. 76–79.

Galerie Nina Dausset, Paris, November 19–December 15, 1954, *Alechinsky*. Text by Christian Dotremont.

Kenan, Amos. *Les Tireurs de Langue*, Turin, Fratelli Pozzo, n.d. [1962] [Alechinsky illustrations].

Galerie de France, Paris, May 2–28, 1962, *Alechinsky*. Text by Jean-François Renal.

Stedelijk Museum, Amsterdam, January 18–March 4, 1963, *Que d'Encre*. Jacques Putnam interviews Pierre Alechinsky.

HORST ANTES

1936, Heppenheim, Germany. State Academy of Fine Arts, Karlsruhe. First one-man exhibition, Galerie der Spiegel, Cologne, 1960. Resident Karlsruhe.

Wedewer, Rolf. "Westfälische Austellungen", *Kunstwerk*, Baden-Baden, vol. 14, no. 12, June, 1961, pp. 43–45. [Review of *Junge Westen* exhibition at Recklinghausen.]

Third Paris Biennale, Musée d'Art Moderne, Paris, September 28–November 3, 1963, *Sonderausstellung Horst Antes*. Text by Herbert Pée.

Linfert, Carlo. *Junge Künstler*, Cologne, 1963.

FRANCIS BACON

1910, Dublin. First one-man exhibition, Hanover Gallery, London, 1949. Most recent one-man exhibitions, Marlborough Fine Art Ltd., London and The Solomon R. Guggenheim Museum, New York, 1963. Resident London.

The Solomon R. Guggenheim Museum, New York, October 17, 1963–January 12, 1964, *Francis Bacon*. Text by Lawrence Alloway. [bibliography]

OLLE BAERTLING

1911, Halmstad, Sweden. Started to paint, 1938; studied with André Lhote and Fernand Léger, 1948. Met Herbin, 1950. Joined Galerie Denise René, 1952. Retrospective exhibition Stockholm, Museum of Modern Art, 1961. Resident Stockholm.

Baertling, Olle. "Den aktuelle Konstens problematik", *Konstperspectiv*, Gothenburg, no. 1, 1958.

Liljevalchs Konsthall, Stockholm, March–April, 1956, *Baertling, Jacobsen, Mortensen*. "Baertling Malerei, 1950–1955", by Oscar Reutersvärd.

Galerie Denise René, Paris, March, 1958, *Baertling, Dramaturge des Formes*. Text by Oscar Reutersvärd.

Moderna Museet and The Swedish Institute, Stockholm, 1961, *Baertling Retrospective Exhibition*. Texts by Teddy Brunius, Oscar Reutersvärd, and Bo Wennberg. [In English; bibliography]

Galerie Denise René, Paris, March–April, 1962, *Baertling*. Text by Alberto Sartoris.

Galerie Hybler, Copenhagen, February–March, 1963, *Baertling*. Text by Sigurd Schultz. [bibliography]

BALTHUS

1908, Paris. Self-taught, but parents painted and Bonnard and Derain were family friends. One-man exhibition Galerie Pierre, Paris, 1934; Pierre Matisse Gallery, New York, 1963. Director, French Academy, Rome. Resident Rome.

Soby, James Thrall. "Balthus", *The Museum of Modern Art Bulletin*, New York, vol. 24, no. 3, 1956–57. [Issued as a catalogue of Balthus exhibition, December 19, 1956–February 3, 1957. Bibliography.]

Pierre Matisse Gallery, New York, March, 1962, *Balthus; Paintings, 1929–1961*. Text by Jacques Lassaigne.

ARNOLD BELKIN

1930, Calgary, Canada. Vancouver School of Art, 1944–47; Banff School of Fine Arts, 1945; La Esmeralda School of Painting and Sculpture, 1948; National Polytechnical Institute, Mexico, 1948–51. One-man exhibition Anglo-American Cultural Institute, Mexico, 1952. Founder and co-editor of *Nueva Presencia*; illustrator, stage-designer. Resident Mexico.

Zora's Gallery, Los Angeles, March–April, 1963, *Arnold Belkin*. Text by the artist.

MAX BILL

1908, Winterthur. Kuntsgewerbeschule, Zürich, 1924–27; Bauhaus, Dessau, with Kandinsky, Klee, Albers and others, 1927–29, 1932–36, member *Abstraction-Création*, Paris. One-man exhibition Galerie des Eaux-vives, Zürich, 1946. Co-founder Hochschule für Gestaltung, Ulm; Director 1951–56. Resident Zürich.

Bill, Max, "The Mastery of Space", *XXe Siècle*, Paris, vol. 2, no. 1, 1939, pp. 50–54.

Bill, Max. *Form: Eine Bilanz über die Formentwicklung um die Mitte des XX Jahrhunderts*, Basel, Karl Werner, 1952. [Includes English translation.]

Rogers, Ernesto. "Max Bill", *Magazine of Art*, Washington, D.C., vol. 46, no. 5, May, 1953, pp. 226–230.

Maldonado, Tomás. *Max Bill*, Buenos Aires, Nueva Visión, 1955. [Primarily writings by the artist; text in Spanish, English, German; bibliography.]

Grohmann, Will. "Max Bill und die Synthese", *Werk*, Zürich, vol. 44, no. 7, July, 1957, pp. 247–254.

Netter, Maria. "Experimente mit Form und Farbe: Bilder und Plastiken von Max Bill", *Quadrum*, Brussels, no. 3, 1957, pp. 79–86.

Gomringer, Eugen, ed. *Max Bill*, Teufen, Niggli, 1958. Texts by Max Bense, Will Grohmann, Richard Lohse, Ernesto Rogers, Ernst Scheidegger, etc.

Staber, Margit. "Max Bill und die Umweltgestaltung", *Zodiac*, Milan, no. 9, 1962, pp. 60–95.

Bense, Max. "Max Bill", *Art International*, Zürich, vol. 7, no. 3, March 25, 1963, pp. 30–35.

BRAM BOGART

1921, Delft. Exhibition, Bennewitz Gallery, The Hague, 1943. One-man exhibition, Galerie Creuze, Paris, 1954. Resident Brussels.

Galleria l'Attico, Rome, November, 1959, *Bogart*. Text by Maurizio Calvesi.

G[aly]—C[arles], H[enry]. "Milan: Bram Bogart", *Aujourd'hui*, Boulogne-sur-Seine, vol. 5, no. 27, June, 1960, p. 53.

Galleria l'Attico, Rome, October–November, 1960, *Bogart*. Text by Jean Dypréau.

LUIGI BOILLÉ

1926, Rome. 1950, degree in painting from Academia di Belle Arti, Rome, in architecture from University of Rome. 1951 to Paris. 1955, one-man exhibition, Galerie Lucien Durand, Paris. Resident Paris.

Galleria d'Arte Selecta, Rome, June 11–20, 1957, *Boillé*. Text by Edouard Jaguer.

Galleria del Naviglio, Milan, November 16–29, 1957, *Luigi Boillé*. Text by Guido Ballo.

Il Giorno, Milan, April 20–May 16, 1958, *Giovanni Artisti Italiani*, pp. 25–26.

C[hevalier], D[enys]. "Boillé", *Aujourd'hui*, Boulogne-sur-Seine, vol. 5, no. 30, February, 1961, p. 46.

JACOBO BORGES

1931, Caracas. School of Plastic Arts of Caracas.

Instituto Cultural Venezolano–Israeli, New York, March 15–31, 1962, *17 Venezuelan Painters*. Text by Miguel C. Arroyo.

GIUSEPPE CAPOGROSSI

1900, Rome. In Paris 1927–33. Co-founder *Gruppo Romano* and *Origine*. First one-man exhibition, 1928, Rome. Professor, Academy of Fine Arts, Rome. Resident Rome.

Capogrossi, Giuseppe. [Statement], in Ritchie, Andrew, ed., *The New Decade: 22 European Painters and Sculptors*, New York, Museum of Modern Art, pp. 86–87.

Seuphor, Michel. *Capogrossi*, Venice, Cavallino, 1954.

Giani, Renato. "Capogrossi o la pitture cerimoniale", *I 4 Soli*, Turin, vol. 1, no. 4–5, July–September, 1954, pp. 6–7.

Matta. "Giuseppe Capogrossi", *I 4 Soli*, Turin, vol. 4, no. 2, March–April, 1957, p. 12.

Argan, G. C. "Capogrossi", *XXe Siècle*, Paris, vol. 20, no. 9, June, 1957, pp. 41–43. [Reprint in Capogrossi catalogue Palais des Beaux-Arts, Brussels, 1959.]

Kochnitzky, Leon. "Giuseppe Capogrossi", *Quadrum*, Brussels, no. 10, 1961, pp. 111–118.

San Lazzaro, G. di. "Capogrossi: ou l'obsession de l'espace", *XXe Siècle*, Paris, vol. 24, no. 18, February, 1962, pp. 42–47.

ENRICO CASTELLANI

1930, Castelmassa (Rovigo), Italy. Architectural degree, École Nationale Supérieure de la Cambre, Brussels, 1956; lived in Brussels, 1952–56. Co-founder of periodical, *Azimuth*. Member of *Nero* and *Nul* groups; contributor to their magazines. Resident Milan.

Castellani, Enrico. [Statement], *Monochrome Malerei*, Städtisches Museum, Leverkusen, March 18–May 8, 1960, pp. 3–4. [in English]

Leisberg, Alexander. "Neue Tendenzen", *Kuntswerk*, Baden-Baden, vol. 14, no. 11, April–May, 1961, pp. 3–34.

Morschel, Jürgen. "Avantgarde 61: Städtische Museum Trier", *Kunstwerk*, Baden-Baden, vol. 14, no. 5–6, November–December, 1961, p. 71.

Thwaites, John Anthony. "Reaching the Zero Zone", *Arts*, New York, vol. 36, no. 10, September, 1962, pp. 16–21.
Galleria dell'Ariete, Milan, February 26, 1963–?, *Castellani*. Text by Gillo Dorfles.

CORNEILLE (Cornelis van Beverloo)

1922, Belgium. State Academy of Fine Arts, Amsterdam. 1948, co-founder *Reflex* group. 1951, co-founder *Cobra* group. First one-man exhibition, 1946. Resident Paris.

Corneille. "Rondom de Hostudstill ungen Denemarken", *Reflex*, no. 2, 1948. [unpaginated]
Dotremont, Christian. *Corneille*, Copenhagen, Bibliothèque de Cobra, 1950.
Stedelijk Museum, Amsterdam, 1956, *Corneille*. Text by Edouard Jaguer.
Minneapolis Institute of Arts, Minneapolis, 1959, *European Art Today*. Text by James Fitzsimmons, "France, Switzerland, the Low Countries, Denmark".
Gemeentemuseum, The Hague, July 14–September 3, 1961, *Corneille*. Text by A. M. Hammacher.

GRAHAM COUGHTRY

1931, St. Lambert, Quebec. Montreal Museum of Fine Arts; Ontario College of Art. First one-man show, Isaacs Gallery, Toronto, 1956.

Fulford, Robert. "Coughtry", *Canadian Art*, Ottawa, vol. 18, no. 1, January–February, 1961, pp. 20–21.
Kilbourn, Elizabeth. "Graham Coughtry at the Isaacs Gallery, Toronto", *Canadian Art*, Ottawa, vol. 19, no. 2, March, 1962, p. 100.

MODEST CUIXART

1925, Barcelona. Academie Libre d'Art, Barcelona. 1948 founding member group and review *Dau al Set*. First one-man exhibition, Amics de les Arts, Barcelona, 1955. Most recent one-man show, Galeria René Métras, Barcelona, 1963. Resident Barcelona.

Cirlot, Juan Eduardo. *La Peinture de Modest Cuixart*, Paris, René Drouin, 1958. "De 1943 à 1958" by René Drouin; "Un peintre espagnol à St. Jean de Lyons" by Jean-Jacques Lerrant; "Notice bibliographique" by René P. Métras. [bibliography]
Galerie René Drouin, Paris, June, 1958, *Cuixart*. Text by Alexandre Cirici-Pellicer. [bibliography]
Cirlot, Juan Eduardo. "La pintura de Modesto Cuixart", *Art International*, Zürich, vol. 3, no. 10, 1959–60, pp. 41–44.
Chueca Goitia, Fernando. "El pintor Modesto Cuixart", *Correo de las Artes*, Barcelona, vol. 4, no. 25, May–June, 1960. [unpaginated]
Lerrant, Jean-Jacques. *Modest Cuixart; Sept Personnages d'Exorcisme*, Paris, René Drouin, 1962.
Grohmann, Will. "Cuixart", *Das Kunstwerk*, Krefeld, vol. 7, no. 15, January, 1962, pp. 3–10.
Restany, Pierre. "Un art du dedans; la peinture de Cuixart", *Cimaise*, Paris, vol. 9, no. 58, March–April, 1962, pp. 70–77. [Text also in English, German, Spanish.]

ERNESTO DEIRA

1928, Buenos Aires. First one-man show Galerias Witcomb, Buenos Aires, 1960. With Galería Bonino, Buenos Aires.

Museo Nacional de Bellas Artes, Buenos Aires, June 15–July 7, 1963, *Deira, Macció, Noé, de la Vega*. Text by Jorge Romero Brest.

PAUL DELVAUX

1897, Antheit-les-Huys, Belgium. Académie des Beaux-Arts, Brussels. 1924, *Le Sillon* group. Teacher Institut National Supérieur d'Architecture et des Arts Décoratifs. Latest one-man exhibition in New York, Staempfli Gallery, 1963. Resident Brussels.

Langui, Émile. *Paul Delvaux*, Venice, Editore Alfieri, 1949.
Langui, Émile. "Les peintures murales de Paul Delvaux chez G. Perier à Bruxelles", *Quadrum*, Brussels, no. 1, May, 1956, pp. 132–142.
Genaille, Robert. *La Peinture en Belgique de Rubens aux Surréalistes*, Paris, Éditions Pierre Tisné, 1958, pp. 143–149.
Jean, Marcel. *Histoire de la Peinture Surréaliste*, Paris, Éditions du Seuil, 1959, pp. 274–278.

JEAN DUBUFFET

1901, Le Havre. After giving up painting for ten years, he resumed painting in 1934–37; then went back to the wholesale wine business he had founded. Exclusively a painter since 1942. First exhibition René Drouin Gallery, Paris, 1944. Trips to the Sahara, 1947–49. Retrospective exhibition, The Museum of Modern Art, New York, 1962. Resident Paris and Vence.

[The first four items refer to Dubuffet's urban imagery.]
Ponge, Francis. *Matière et Mémoire ou les lithographes à l'école*, Paris, 1944. [lithographs by Jean Dubuffet]
Parrot, Louis. *Jean Dubuffet*, Paris, 1944.
Guillevec. *Les Murs*, Paris, 1950. [executed c. 1945] [lithographs by Jean Dubuffet]
Paulhan, Jean. *La Metromanie ou les derrous de la capitale*, Paris, 1950. [drawings by Jean Dubuffet]
Musée des Arts Décoratifs, Paris, 1960, *Jean Dubuffet 1942–60*. Includes "Mémoir sur le développement de mes travaux depuis 1952" by Dubuffet. [bibliography]
The Museum of Modern Art, New York, February 21–April 8, 1962, *The Work of Jean Dubuffet*. Texts by Peter Selz and Dubuffet, including "Memoir on the Development of my Work from 1952", translation of article in Musée des Arts Décoratifs catalogue above. [bibliography]
Galerie Daniel Cordier, Paris, June 7–?, 1962; Cordier and Ekstrom Gallery, New York, November 20–December 29, 1962. *Dubuffet; Paris Circus*.

ÖYVIND FAHLSTRÖM

1928, São Paolo. Stockholm since 1939. Istituto Svedese, Rome, 1955, 1957, 1959, studying Pre-Columbian Codices Vaticanus. Facsimile artist for Swedish University Libraries. One-man exhibition Galleria Numero, Florence, 1952; Galerie Daniel Cordier, Paris, 1959, 1962. Has published plays, poetry, criticism. Member *Phases*. Resident New York.

Wretholm, Eugen. "Bilden Encyklopedisten Öyvind Fahlström", *Konstrevy*, Stockholm, vol. 34, no. 1, 1958, pp. 20–22.
Galerie, Daniel Cordier, Paris, February 19–March 15, 1959, *Öyvind Fahlström*. Text by Edouard Jaguer.
Hultén, K. G. "Öyvind Fahlström", *Quadrum*, Brussels, no. 8, 1960, pp. 150–151.
Galerie Daniel Cordier, Paris, December 6, 1962–January 12, 1963, *Öyvind Fahlström*. Text by Robert Rauschenberg.

WOJCIECH FANGOR

1922, Warsaw. Academy of Fine Arts, Warsaw, 1946. Taught at Academy of Fine Arts, Warsaw. Exhibitions in Europe since 1949. Resident Montrouge, France.

The Museum of Modern Art, New York, August 3–October 1, 1961, *15 Polish Painters*. Text by Peter Selz.

JOSÉ A. FERNÁNDEZ-MURO

1920, Madrid. Moved to Argentina, 1938; Argentine citizen. First one-man exhibition in United States, Pan American Union, Washington, D.C., 1957. With Galería Bonino, Buenos Aires, 1962.

Andrew-Morris Gallery, New York, February 15–March 9, 1963, *Fernández-Muro*. Text by Cleve Gray.
Institute of Contemporary Art, Boston, Exhibition Circulating 1961–62, *Latin America: New Departures*. Statement by the artist.

LUCIO FONTANA

1899, Rosario di Santa Fé, Argentina. 1905, moved to Milan. Brera Academy. First exhibition abstract sculpture at Galleria del Milione, Milan, 1930; member *Abstraction-Création*, Paris, 1934. 1939–46 in Argentina. Published *Manifesto Blanco*, Buenos Aires, 1946. Returned to Milan, 1947. Founded *Spacialist* movement, published *Manifesto Spaziale*. Exhibitions at Galleria del Naviglio, Milan, since 1949. Resident Milan.

Fontana, Lucio. "Technical Manifesto Given at the First International Congress of Proportion at the IXth Triennale, Milan, 1947", *Ark*, London, no. 24, 1959, pp. 4–7. [Commentary by Lawrence Alloway] Also published Conchiglia, Milan, 1959.
Giani, Giampiero. *Fontana*, Venice, Cavallino, 1958. [Text excerpt from Giani, *Spazialismo*, Milan, Conchiglia, 1956.]
Galleria l'Attico, Rome, October, 1959, *Fontana*. Text by Enrico Crispolti.
Oliver, Paul. "Lucio Fontana", *Art International*, Zürich, vol. 6, no. 2, March, 1962, pp. 37–40.
Ballo, Guido. *Continuità*, Milan, Galleria Levi, 1962. [Text in Italian, French, English. Published on occasion of exhibition of *Continuità* group, June, 1962.]
Tapié, Michel. *Fontana*, New York, Abrams, 1962.

ALBERTO GIACOMETTI

1901, Stampa, Switzerland. Studied with his father, Giovanni Giacometti, to 1915; 1919, School of Arts and Crafts, Geneva; 1922, with Archipenko, Paris; 1922–24, Académie de la Grande Chaumière under Bourdelle. 1930–32 member Surrealist group. One-man exhibition Galerie Pierre Colle, Paris, 1932; Galerie Krugier, Geneva, 1963. Resident Paris.

Giacometti, Alberto. "The Dream, The Sphinx, The Death of T", *X*, London, vol. 1, no. 1, 1959. [First published in French in *Labyrinthe*, Geneva, vol. 22–23, December, 1946, pp. 12–13.]
Alberto Giacometti: Schriften, Fotos, Zeichnungen, Zürich, Arche, 1958. [Text in French and German.]
Hess, Thomas B. "Giacometti: The Uses of Adversity", *Art News*, New York, vol. 57, no. 3, May, 1958, pp. 34–35, 67. [The account of an interview in Paris.]
Dupin, Jacques. *Alberto Giacometti*, Paris, Maeght, 1962.
Bucarelli, Palma. *Giacometti*, Rome, Editalia, 1962. [Text in Italian, French, English; bibliography.]
Genêt, Jean. *Alberto Giacometti*, Zürich, Ernst Scheidegger, 1962. [Primarily in the form of an extensive interview with the artist.]

Kunsthaus, Zürich, December 2, 1962–January 6, 1963, *Alberto Giacometti*. Texts by Rene Wehrli, Eduard Hüttinger; excerpts from texts by Sartre and Giacometti.
Derrière le Miroir, Paris [Maeght], Special issues on Giacometti: no. 39–40, June–July, 1951; no. 65, May, 1954; no. 98, June, 1957; no. 127, May, 1961. Texts by Michel Leiris, Jean-Paul Sartre, Jean Genêt, Olivier Larronde, Léna Leclerq, Isaku Yanaihara; some of which reprinted in above entries.

ADOLPH GOTTLIEB

1903, New York City. Art Students League, New York. 1920–23, with John Sloan, Robert Henri. First one-man exhibition, Dudensing Galleries, New York, 1930. Taught at Pratt Institute, New York and U.C.L.A., Los Angeles, 1958. With Sidney Janis Gallery, New York. Most recent exhibition, Walker Art Center, Minneapolis, 1963. Resident New York City.

Galerie Rive Droite, Paris, 1959, *Gottlieb: École de New York*. Text by Clement Greenberg.
Walker Art Center, Minneapolis, 1963, *Adolph Gottlieb*. Text by Martin Friedman. [bibliography]

GUNNAR GUNDERSEN

1921, Förde, Sunnfjord, Norway. School of Industrial Arts and Crafts, Oslo; Norwegian Academy of Arts, Oslo. Most recent one-man show, Galleri Haaken, Oslo, March–April, 1963. Teaches at School of Architecture, Norwegian School of Technics, Trondheim. Resident Oslo.

The Corcoran Gallery of Art, Washington, D.C., October 6–November 5, 1961 and Munson-Williams-Proctor Institute, Utica, March 4–April 1, 1962, *Eight Painters from Norway*. Text by Jan Askeland.

PHILIP GUSTON

1913, Montreal. 1919, to Los Angeles. 1936, to New York. W. P. A. Federal Arts Project, mural division, 1936–40. First one-man exhibition, State University of Iowa, 1944. First New York exhibition, Midtown Galleries, 1945. Taught drawing, New York University, 1951–59. Joined Sidney Janis Gallery, New York, 1956. Comprehensive exhibition, The Solomon R. Guggenheim Museum, New York, 1962. Resident New York City and Woodstock, New York.

The Solomon R. Guggenheim Museum, New York, May 2–July 1, 1962, *Philip Guston*. Text by H. H. Arnason. [bibliography]
Hunter, Sam. "Philip Guston", *Art International*, Zürich, vol. 6, no. 1, May, 1962, pp. 62–67.
O'Hara, Frank. "Growth and Guston", *Art News*, New York, vol. 61, no. 3, May, 1962, pp. 31–33, 51–52.
Alloway, Lawrence. "Notes on Guston", *College Art Journal*, New York, vol. 22, no. 1, Fall, 1962, pp. 8–11.

VERA HALLER

1910, Budapest. Academie Henri Wabel, Zürich, 1949–50. First one-man exhibition, Zum Strauhoff, Zürich, 1954; exhibition at Zoe Dusanne Gallery, Seattle, 1958. Swiss citizen; resident Zürich.

C[ampbell], L[awrence]. "Vera Haller", *Art News*, New York, vol. 52, no. 5, September, 1953, p. 55.
Fitzsimmons, James. "Art: Vera Haller", *Arts and Architecture*, Los Angeles, vol. 73, no. 12, December, 1956, p. 10.

Minneapolis Institute of Arts, Minneapolis, September 23–October 25, 1959, *European Art Today: 35 Painters and Sculptors.* Text on Haller by James Fitzsimmons, pp. 26–28, 77.

ICA Gallery, London, January 19–February 18, 1961, *Vera Haller, Wolfgang Hollegha.* Text by Lawrence Alloway.

SIMON HANTAÏ

1922, Bia, Hungary. 1941–47 School of Fine Arts, Budapest. To Paris, 1949. First one-man exhibition Galerie L'Étoile Scellée, 1951. Associated with Surrealist group until 1955.

Hantaï, Simon. [Illustrations]. *Medium: communication Surréaliste,* Paris, no. 1, November, 1953. [illustrated by Hantäi throughout; note and biography, p. 1.]

Galerie Kléber, Paris, May 11–June 9, 1956, *Sexe-Prime. Hommage à Jean-Pierre Brisset et autres peintures de Simon Hantaï.* Text a series of quotations chosen by the artist.

Galerie René Drouin, Paris, October, 1956. *Tensions: Georges, Viseux, Reigl, Hantaï, Degottex.* Text by Hubert Damisch.

F[ranca], J.-A. "Hantaï", *Aujourd'hui,* Boulogne-sur-Seine, vol. 8, no. 38, September, 1962, p. 55.

HANS HOFMANN

1880, Weissenburg, Germany. 1898 began study of painting in Munich. In Paris, 1904–14. 1915 opened art school in Munich. To United States, 1930. Taught at Chouinard Art Institute, Los Angeles; University of California, Berkeley; Art Students League, New York; Thurn School, Gloucester, Massachusetts. 1933–34 founded own schools in Provincetown, Massachusetts and New York. First one-man show in New York, Art of this Century, 1944. Regularly exhibits Kootz Gallery, New York. Retrospective exhibition The Museum of Modern Art, 1963. Resident New York City.

"Repertory of Means: 'Bald Eagle' by Hans Hofmann", *Location,* New York, vol. 1, no. 1, Spring, 1963, pp. 67–72. Photographs by Rudolph Burkhardt.

Seitz, William C. *Hans Hofmann,* New York, Museum of Modern Art, 1963. With selected writings by the artist. [bibliography]

WOLFGANG HOLLEGHA

1929, Klagenfurt, Austria. Akademie des Bildenden Künste, Vienna. One-man exhibition Art Club, Vienna, 1953; Galerie St. Stephan, Vienna, 1963. Resident Vienna.

B[utler], B[arbara]. "Wolfgang Hollegha", *Arts,* New York, vol. 34, no. 9, June, 1960, pp. 58–59.

Galerie St. Stephan, Vienna, and Galerie 55, Aschaffenburg, 1960, *Neue Österreichische Kunst.* Text by Otto Mauer.

ICA Gallery, London, January 19–February 18, 1961, *Vera Haller, Wolfgang Hollegha.* Text by Lawrence Alloway.

Hofmann, Werner. "Hollegha", *Quadrum,* Brussels, no. 11, pp. 148–149.

GOTTFRIED HONEGGER

1917, Zürich. School for Arts and Crafts, Zürich. Resident Paris and Zürich.

Honegger, Gottfried. *Illuminationen,* Zürich, Girsberger, 1950. [9 lithographs; text by Selma Regula Gessner.]

Honegger, Gottfried. *Transmissions,* New York, Wittenborn, 1954. [7 lithographs; texts by Katherine Kuh and Willy Rotzler.]

Martha Jackson Gallery, New York, February 27–March 19, 1960. *Honegger.* Text by Aleksis Rannit.

Read, Herbert. "Gottfried Honegger", *Letter to a Young Painter,* New York, Horizon Press, 1962, pp. 128–129.

Gimpel and Hanover Galerie, Zürich, January 25–March 10, 1963, *Honegger.* Texts by Herbert Read [reprint of above] and Michel Seuphor.

FRITZ HUNDERTWASSER (Friederich Stowasser)

1928, Vienna. Akademie der Bildenden Künste, Vienna, 1948. One-man exhibition Art Club of Vienna, 1952. 1953–56, Paris. 1959, taught one month at Akademie der Bildenden Künste, Hamburg. Resident Vienna.

Lacoste, Michel Conil. "Conversation dans l'atelier 2: Hundertwasser", *L'Oeil,* Paris, no. 74, February, 1961, pp. 46–51. [Interview]

Galerie Anne Abels, Cologne, May 18–June 22, 1963, *Hundertwasser ist ein Geschenk fur Deutchland. . . .* Text by the artist.

Ankwicz von Kleehoven, Hans. "Fritz Hundertwasser", *Kunstwerk,* Baden-Baden, vol. 10, no. 5, 1956–57, pp. 43–45, 50.

Restany, Pierre. *Hundertwasser,* Paris, H. Kamer, 1957. [Published in conjunction with exhibition at Galerie Kamer, March, 1957. Texts by the artist pp. 10–18.]

Jouffroy, Alain. "Curieuse aventure d'une spirale à Hambourg", *Arts,* Paris, no. 764, March 2–8, 1960, pp. 1, 4.

Choay, Françoise. "Le temps et les sentiers de la folie chez Hundertwasser", *Quadrum,* Brussels, no. 14, 1963, pp. 71–78.

FRANCISCO ICAZA

1930, in Mexican Embassy in Central America. Academy of Fine Arts, Brussels. First one-man show, Galeria del Caballito, 1956, Mexico City. Since 1952 resident Mexico.

Nelken, Margarita. "Nuevos aspectos de la plastica Mexicana", *Artes de Mexico,* vol. 9, no. 33, 1961, p. 47.

EGILL JACOBSEN

1910, Copenhagen. Royal Academy of Fine Arts, Copenhagen. First exhibition, 1932, Copenhagen. Founding member *Cobra* group. Since 1959, professor at Royal Academy of Fine Arts, Copenhagen. Resident Copenhagen.

Olsen, R. Dahlmann. "Egill Jacobsen", *Helhesten,* Copenhagen, vol. 1, no. 2, n.d. [1941–1943], pp. 40–43.

Dotremont, Christian. *Egill Jacobsen,* Copenhagen, Bibliothèque de Cobra, 1950.

Charlottenborg, December 7–18, 1960, *Egill Jacobsen; Retrospective Udstilling.* Text by Ejner Johannson, exhibition arranged by Kunstnernes Kunsthandel, Copenhagen.

Maison du Danemark, Paris, January 14–July 5, 1962, *Egill Jacobsen; Retrospective.*

Dotremont, Christian. *Jacobsen-Malerier fra 1962,* Copenhagen, n.d.

ALAIN JACQUET

1939, Neuilly sur Seine, France. Exhibited Galerie Bretau since 1959. Resident Paris.

S[imone], F[rigério]. "Jacquet", *Aujourd'hui,* Boulogne-sur-Seine, vol. 8, no. 38, p. 55.

ASGER JORN

1914, Jutland, Denmark. Worked with Léger, Le Corbusier, Paris, 1936–37. Founding member *Cobra* group, 1948–51; later International Movement for a Bauhaus Imaginist. 1948, first one-man exhibition Galerie Breteau, Paris. 1962, first one-man exhibition in United States, Lefebre Gallery, New York. Resident Paris.

Jorn, Asger. *Pour la Forme*, Paris, n.d. [1958] [Collection of texts written 1954–57.]

Jorn, Asger. *Guldhorn og Lykkehjul*, Copenhagen, Bogtrykkeriet Selandia, Als, n.d. [unpaginated]. [French translation: *La Roue de la Fortune*.]

Dotremont, Christian. *Asger Jorn*, Copenhagen, no. 14, Bibliothèque de Cobra, 1950.

Galerie Birch, Copenhagen, n.d. *Drømmebilledet*. [Paintings 1954–55.]

Haftmann, Werner. "Asger Jorn", *Quadrum*, Brussels, no. 12, 1961, pp. 61–84. [English resumé, 190–192.]

Ragon, Michel. "Asger Jorn", *Cimaise*, Paris, vol. 7, no. 1, January–February, 1961, pp. 48–57.

MINORU KAWABATA

1911, Tokyo. Graduated Tokyo Academy of Fine Arts, 1934; 1939–41 in France, Italy. One-man exhibition, Mitsukoshi Art Gallery, Tokyo, 1940. Taught Tama University, Tokyo, 1950–55; New School for Social Research, New York, 1958–61. Exhibitions Betty Parsons Gallery, New York, 1960, 1961, 1963. Resident New York.

C[ampbell], L[awrence]. "Kawabata", *Art News*, New York, vol. 59, no. 1, March, 1960, p. 19.

T[illim], S[idney]. "Kawabata", *Arts*, New York, vol. 34, no. 7, April, 1960, p. 66.

C[ampbell], L[awrence]. "Kawabata", *Art News*, New York, vol. 60, no. 4, Summer, 1961, p. 52.

R. B. KITAJ

1932, Ohio. 1950, Cooper Union, New York, under Delevante, Dowden, Zucker, and Ferren; 1951, Academy of Fine Art, Vienna; 1958–61, Ruskin School of Drawing, Oxford; Royal College of Art, London. 1962 drawing master, Ealing School of Art and Camberwell School of Art, London. One-man exhibition Marlborough New London Gallery, London, 1963. Resident London.

Marlborough Fine Art Ltd., London, February, 1963, *R. B. Kitaj, Pictures with Commentary, Pictures without Commentary.* Text by the artist.

WILLEM DE KOONING

1904, Rotterdam. 1916 apprenticed to firm of decorators; 1919 to painter Bernard Romein. Academie van Beeldende Kunsten, Rotterdam, c. 1920. Moved to New York City, 1926. First one-man exhibition, Egan Gallery, New York, 1948. Regularly exhibits Sidney Janis Gallery, New York. Most recent exhibition, Allan Stone Gallery, New York, 1962. Resident New York.

de Kooning, Willem. "Content Is a Glimpse . . .", *Location*, New York, no. 1, Spring, 1963, pp. 53–65. [Published here as a monologue, but originally an interview with David Sylvester, "Painting as Self-Discovery", broadcast by BBC, London, December 30, 1960.]

Sketchbook 1: Three Americans, Time Inc., 1960, pp. 1–2, 5–10. Film script in interview form.

Hess, Thomas B. *Willem de Kooning*, New York, Braziller, 1959. [bibliography]

Janis, Harriet; Blesh, Rudi. *De Kooning*, New York, Grove Press, 1960.

Sidney Janis Gallery, New York, March 5–31, 1962, *de Kooning*. Text by Thomas B. Hess. [Deals with 1959–61 works.]

Rosenberg, Harold. "Painting as a Way of Living", *New Yorker*, New York, February 16, 1963.

WIFREDO LAM

1902, Sagua La Grande, Cuba. Studied in Havana, Madrid, Barcelona. First one-man exhibition 1932, Spain. To Paris, 1938. Most recent one-man show, Albert Loeb Gallery, New York, 1962. Resident Albisola Mare, Italy.

Ortiz, Fernando. *Wifredo Lam*, Havana, Publicationes del Ministerio de Education, 1950. Series: Cuadernos de Arte, 1.

Charpier, Jacques. *Lam*, Paris, Le Musée de Poche, 1960. [bibliography]

Lebel, Robert. "Wifredo Lam and the Recovery of Exoticism", *Figures*, New York, vol. 9, 1961, pp. 32–37.

Tarnaud, Claude. "Wifredo Lam et la bestiaire ambigu", *XXe Siècle*. Paris, vol. 25, no. 21, May, 1963, pp. 37–42.

RICHARD P. LOHSE

1902, Zürich. School of Arts and Crafts, Zürich, 1920–24. Cofounder Association of Modern Swiss Architects, 1936. One-man exhibition Club Bel Étage, Zürich, 1957; Kunsthaus, Zürich, 1962. Resident Zürich.

Lohse, Richard P. "A Revised Thematic for Progressive Art", *Trans/formation*, New York, vol. 1, no. 3, 1952, pp. 163–164.

Gerstner, Karl. *Kalte Kunst? Zum Standort der heutigen Malerei*, Teufen, Niggli, 1957.

Galerie Charles Lienhard, Zürich, 1960, *Der Maler Richard P. Lohse*. Texts by Hans Neuberg and the artist.

Richard P. Lohse, Teufen, Niggli, 1962. Texts by Pasmore, Vantongerloo, Bill, W. Sandberg, and others.

Neuburg, Hans: "Der Bildraum und seine Gesetze: Zur Malerei von Richard P. Lohse, Erweiterte Wiedergabe eines Artikeis aus der Zeitschrift *Werk*", *Neue Grafik*, Zürich, no. 12, March, 1962, pp. 2–22 [Text also in French, English]

Kunsthaus, Zürich, September 21–October 21, 1962, *Richard P. Lohse*. Introduction by R. W.; "Entwicklungslinien 1940/62" by the artist.

LUCEBERT

1924, Amsterdam. School of Applied Arts, Amsterdam. Member *Cobra* and *Reflex* groups. One-man exhibition, Galerie Espace, Haarlem, 1958; Städtische Kunstgalerie, Bochum, 1963. Resident Bergen, Holland.

Stedelijk Museum, Amsterdam, April 17–May 26, 1959, *Lucebert*. Statement by the artist.

Galerie der Spiegel, Cologne, 1960, *Geh durch den Spiegel*. Poems and illustrations by the artist.

Städtische Kunstgalerie, Bochum, May 25–August 21, 1963, *Lucebert*. Statement by the artist.

EVERT LUNDQUIST

1904, Stockholm. Studied with Carl Wilhelmson; Académie Julian, Paris, 1924–25; Royal Academy of Fine Arts, Stockholm, 1925–31. One-man exhibition, Stockholm, 1934. Leader *Saltsjö-Duvnäs* group. Resident Drottningholm.

Blomberg, Averik. "Evert Lundquist", *Kunsten Idag*, Oslo, vol. 45, no. 3, 1958, pp. 32–51. [English translation pp. 56–59]

Holden, Cliff. "Evert Lundquist", *Art News and Review*, London, vol. 10, no. 25, January 3, 1959, p. 6. [Includes statements by the artist.]

Galerie Rive Gauche, Paris, February, 1960, *Evert Lundquist*. Texts by R. V. Gindertael and Teddy Brunius.

Forge, Andrew. "Painters to Watch: Evert Lundquist", *The Observer*, London, October 23, 1960, p. 33.

Söderberg, Rolf. *Evert Lundquist*, Stockholm, Bonnier's, 1962.

RÓMULO MACCIÓ

1931, Buenos Aires. First one-man exhibition, Buenos Aires, 1956. With Galería Bonino, Buenos Aires. Resident Paris.

Museo Nacional de Bellas Artes, Buenos Aires, June 15–July 7, 1963, *Deira, Macció, Noé, de la Vega*. Text by Jorge Romero Brest.

HEINZ MACK

1931, Dusseldorf. 1950–53, Kunstakademie, Dusseldorf; philosophy degree, University of Cologne, 1956. One-man exhibition, Galerie Schmela, Dusseldorf, 1957; Galeria Cadario, Milan, 1963. Member *Group 53;* Co-founder and editor *Zero*, group and review. Resident Dusseldorf.

Mon, Franz, ed. *Movens*, Wiesbaden, Limes, 1960.

Leisberg, Alexander. "Neue Tendenzen", *Kunstwerk*, Baden-Baden, vol. 14, no. 10–11, April–May, 1961, pp. 3–34.

Moderna Museet, Stockholm, May 17–September 3, 1961, *Rörelse i Konsten*. Catalogue edited by K. G. Hultén, and statement by the artist, p. 24.

Thwaites, John Anthony. "Reaching the Zero Zone", *Arts*, New York, vol. 36, no. 10, September, 1962, pp. 16–21.

Thwaites, John Anthony. "The New German Painting", *Art in America*, New York, vol. 50, no. 3, 1962, pp. 118–123.

RENÉ MAGRITTE

1898, Lessines, Belgium. Académie des Beaux-Arts, Brussels, 1916–18. Association with French Surrealist group. First one-man exhibition, 1927, Galerie Le Centaure, Brussels. Most recent one-man show in New York, Iolas Gallery, 1962. Resident Brussels.

Obelisk Gallery, London, September 28–October 27, 1961. Edited by Philip M. Laski. Appreciations by Arp, Breton and others. [bibliography]

Magritte, René. "Leçon de choses: écrits et dessins de René Magritte" *Rhétorique*, no. 7, October, 1962.

Sidney Janis Gallery, New York, March 1–20, 1954, *The Words Versus the Image*.

Gablik, Suzi. "René Magritte: Mystery Painter", *Harpers Bazaar*, New York, no. 3025, November, 1963, pp. 148–150, 190–191.

MATTA (Roberto Sebastian Antonio Matta Echaurren)

1912, Santiago, Chile. 1933, graduated from School of Architecture, Santiago. Studied architecture, Le Corbusier's office, Paris, 1934–37. 1937 joined Surrealist group, Paris. 1938 began painting. 1939 to New York. First exhibition in New York, Julian Levy Gallery, 1940. One-man exhibition, The Museum of Modern Art, 1957. Most recent exhibition, Museo Civico, Bologna, 1963. Resident Paris.

Galeria del Naviglio, Milan, 1958, *Matta*. Text by Matta.

Rubin, William. "Matta", *The Museum of Modern Art Bulletin*, New York, vol. 25, no. 1, 1957. Issued as catalogue of exhibition, September 10–October 20, 1957. [bibliography]

Galerie Daniel Cordier, Frankfurt, 1959, *Matta*. Text by Will Grohmann.

L'Attico, Rome, November, 1961, *Matta*. Text by Emilio Villa.

JOSEF MIKL

Vienna, 1929. Vienna Kunstakademie under Dobrowsky. One-man exhibition Galleria La Bussola, Turin, 1951; Galerie Der Spiegel, Cologne, Galerie Springer, Berlin, 1963. Resident Vienna.

Schmidt, Georg. *Neue Malerie in Österreich*, Vienna, Brüder Rosenbaum, 1956.

Grohmann, Will. "Germany, Austria, Switzerland", *Art Since 1945*, New York, Abrams, 1958, pp. 155–220.

Schmeller, A. "Josef Mikl", *Quadrum*, Brussels, no. 8, 1960, pp. 158–159.

Galerie St. Stephan, Vienna, and Galerie 55, Aschaffenburg, 1960, *Neue Österreichische Kunst*. Text by Otto Mauer.

JOAN MIRÓ

1893, Montroig, near Barcelona. School of Fine Arts, Barcelona, 1907–1910; Academy Gali, Barcelona, 1912–15. 1918, first one-man exhibition, Galerie Dalman, Barcelona. 1919 to Paris. 1922, exhibited in international Dada exhibition. 1925 exhibited in first Surrealist show, Paris. Retrospective exhibition, The Museum of Modern Art, New York, 1959. Most recent exhibition, with Artigas, Galerie Maeght, Paris, 1963. Resident Palma, Majorca.

Zervos, Christian et al. "L'Oeuvre de Joan Miró de 1917 à 1933", *Cahiers d'Art*, nos. 1–4, 1934, pp. 11–58.

Greenberg, Clement. *Joan Miró*, New York, Quadrangle Press, 1948.

Erben, Walter. *Joan Miró*, New York, Braziller, 1959.

Soby, James Thrall. *Joan Miró*, New York, Museum of Modern Art, 1959.

Rubin, William. "Miró in Retrospect", *Art International*, Zürich, vol. 3, nos. 5–6, 1959, pp. 34–41.

Dupin, Jacques. *Miró*, Cologne, Du Mont Schauberg, 1961. [bibliography]

Pierre Matisse Gallery, New York, October 31–November 23, 1961, *Miró 1959–1960*. Text by Yvon Taillandier.

GUIDO MOLINARI

1933, Montreal. École des Beaux-Arts, Montreal. Founder and director *L'Actuelle*, art gallery. First one-man show, L'Échourie Gallery, Montreal, 1954. Latest exhibition, East Hampton Gallery, New York, 1962.

Tillim, Sidney. "Exhibition at East Hampton Gallery", *Arts*, New York, vol. 37, February, 1963, p. 54.

J[ill] J[ohnston]. "Exhibition at East Hampton Gallery", *Art News*, New York, vol. 61, January, 1963, p. 18.

RICHARD MORTENSEN

1910, Copenhagen. Royal Academy, Copenhagen, 1931–33. Settled in Paris, 1947. First one-man exhibition, Tokanten Gallery, Copenhagen, 1946. Since 1949, has exhibited regularly at Galerie Denise René, Paris. Resident Paris.

Habasque, Guy. "Les expositions: Mortensen et Vasarely", *Art d'Aujourd'hui*, Paris, vol. 2, no. 11, January, 1957.

XXX Venice Biennale, 1960, "Richard Mortensen", pp. 209–212. Text by Jorn Rubon.

Johanssen, Ejnar. "Richard Mortensen", *Art International*, Zürich, vol. 4, no. 6, June 10, 1960, pp. 49–52.

Galerie Denise René, Paris, June, 1962, *Richard Mortensen*. [bibliography]

ROBERT MOTHERWELL

1915, Aberdeen, Washington. Otis Art Institute, Los Angeles, 1926–27; California School of Fine Arts, San Francisco, 1932; Stanford University (B.A. in Philosophy), 1936; Harvard University Graduate School, 1937–38; University of Grenoble, France, 1939; Columbia University, 1940. First one-man exhibition, Art of this Century, New York, 1944. Most recent exhibition, Smith College Museum of Art, Northampton, Massachusetts, 1963. Resident New York City.

Pasadena Art Museum, February 16–March 11, 1962, *Robert Motherwell, A Retrospective Exhibition*. Foreword by Thomas W. Leavitt; "Robert Motherwell" by Frank O'Hara; "Robert Motherwell's Collages" by Sam Hunter; "All elegies are black and white", poem by Barbara Guest; "What Should a Museum Be" by Robert Motherwell.

Smith College Museum of Art, Northampton, Massachusetts, January 10–28, 1963, *Robert Motherwell*. With "A Conversation at Lunch" by Motherwell. [bibliography]

HENRY MUNDY

1919, Birkenhead, England. Laird School of Art, Birkenhead, 1933–37; Camberwell School of Arts and Crafts, London, 1946–50. First one-man exhibition, Gallery One, London, 1954. Latest one-man exhibition, Hanover Gallery, London, 1962. Teaches at Bath Academy of Art. Resident London.

Mundy, Henry, "Effects Used in Painting", *Gazette*, London, no. 2, 1961, p. 1.

Hanover Gallery, London, September 6–30, 1960, *Mundy*. Text by Alan Bowness.

Alloway, Lawrence. "Henry Mundy", *Art News and Review*, London, vol. 12, no. 18, September 27–October 8, 1960, pp. 4, 14.

Hanover Gallery, London, 1962, *Mundy*. Text by David Sylvester.

Stone Gallery, Newcastle-upon-Tyne, n.d., *Henry Mundy*. Text by Philip James.

TOMOYASU MURAKAMI

1938, Tokyo. Tokyo Art University's "Nihon-ga" (traditional Japanese painting department) 1958–61. First one-man show, Mimatsu Gallery, Tokyo, 1961. Latest exhibition Yoseido Gallery, Tokyo, 1963. Resident Tokyo.

BARNETT NEWMAN

1905, New York City. Art Students League, New York, 1922–26, with John Sloan. 1948, founded with Baziotes, Motherwell and Rothko, the school, *Subjects of the Artist*, later *The Club*. First one-man exhibition, Betty Parsons Gallery, New York, 1950. Retrospective, Bennington College, Bennington, Vermont, 1958. Most recent exhibition Allan Stone Gallery, New York, 1962. Resident New York City.

[It is the purpose of this partial entry to record some of Newman's writing about painting rather than his writing about painters.]

Betty Parsons Gallery, New York, January 20–February 8, 1947, *The Ideographic Picture*. Text by Barnett Newman.

Newman, Barnett B. "The First Man Was an Artist", *Tiger's Eye*, Westport, Conn., no. 1, October, 1947, pp. 57–60.

[Statement] in "The Ides of Art: The Attitudes of 10 Artists on their Work and Contemporaneousness", *Tiger's Eye*, Westport, Conn., no. 2, December, 1947, pp. 42–46.

Newman, Barnett B. "The Object and the Image", *Tiger's Eye*, Westport, Conn., no. 3, March, 1948, p. 111.

[Statement] in "The Ides of Art: 6 Opinions on What is Sublime in Art: The Sublime is Now", *Tiger's Eye*, Westport, Conn., no. 6, December, 1948, pp. 51–53.

[Statement] in *The New American Painting*, New York, Museum of Modern Art, 1958–1959, pp. 60–63.

Seckler, Dorothy Gees. "Frontiers of Space", *Art in America*, New York, vol. 50, no. 2, Summer, 1962, pp. 81–87. [Interview with Barnett Newman]

LUIS FELIPE NOÉ

1933, Buenos Aires. First one-man show, Galerías Witcomb, Buenos Aires, 1959. Exhibits with Galería Bonino, Buenos Aires.

Museo Nacional de Bellas Artes, Buenos Aires, June 15–July 7, 1963, *Deira, Maccío, Noé, de la Vega*. Text by Jorge Romero Brest.

PETER NYBORG

1937, Denmark. Royal Academy of Fine Arts, Copenhagen, with Egill Jacobsen, 1960–62. First one-man exhibition, Copenhagen, 1959. Resident Paris.

Galerie K.-K., Copenhagen, October 27–November 10, 1962, *Peter Nyborg*. Text by Pierre Lübecker. [in Danish]

AVSHALOM OKASHI

1916, Rishon-L'Zion, Israel. Exhibition Haifa Art Gallery, 1954. Resident Acre and The Gallilee, Israel.

Gamzu, Haim. *Painting and Sculpture in Israel*. Tel Aviv, Dvir, 1958, pp. 52–53.

Fischer, Yona. "Les Arts Plastiques en Israël", *Aujourd'hui*, Boulogne-sur-Seine, no. 26, April, 1960, pp. 11–26.

TOSHINOBU ONOSATO

1912, Iida City. Atelier Sefu Tsuda, 1931–33. 1935 exhibited with Nika Society. One-man show Takemiya Gallery, Tokyo, 1953. 1961 one-man exhibition, Gres Gallery, Washington, D.C. Resident Kiryu City.

ALEJANDRO OTERO

1921, Upata, Venezuela. School of Plastic and Applied Arts, Caracas, 1939–45. First one-man exhibition, Ateneo de Valencia, Valencia, Venezuela, 1944. France, 1945–52. Professor, Cristobal Rojas School of Plastic Arts, Caracas, 1954–59. Resident Paris.

Catlin, Stanton L. "New Vistas in Latin American Art", *Art in America*, New York, no. 3, 1959, pp. 24–31.

Messer, Thomas M. "Pan America: Contemporary Idioms", *Art in America*, New York, vol. 49, no. 3, 1961, pp. 88–92.

CARL-HENNING PEDERSEN

1913, Copenhagen. First one-man exhibition, Copenhagen, 1942. Member *Høst* group, 1942–50; founding member *Cobra* group, 1948–51. Most recent one-man show, Galerie de France, Paris, 1963. Resident Copenhagen.

Andreasen, Erik; Pedersen, Carl-Henning. *Universum Fabularum*, Copenhagen, 1957.

Jacobsen, Egill. "Introduktion til Carl-Henning Pedersen's Billeder", *Helhesten*, Copenhagen, 1941–43, pp. 73–75.

Dotremont, Christian. *Carl-Henning Pedersen*, Copenhagen, Bibliothèque de Cobra, 1950.

Nash, Jorgen. "Maleren, Carl-Henning Pedersen", *Konstrevy*, Copenhagen, vol. 30, nos. 5–6, 1955, pp. 226–230.

Galerie de France, Paris, February 15–March 16, 1963, *Carl-Henning Pedersen*. Text by Christian Dotremont.

OTTO PIENE

1928, Laasphe, Germany. High School for Fine Arts, Munich, 1948-50; Kunstakademie, Dusseldorf, 1950–53. 1957-59 member *Group 53;* 1958, editor and co-founder *Zero* review and group. One-man exhibitions Galerie Alfred Schmela, Dusseldorf, regularly since 1959. Resident Dusseldorf.

Piene, Otto. *10 Texte*, Frankfurt, Dato Galerie, April, 1961.

Galerie Diogenes, Berlin, February 20–March 15, 1960, *Piene.* Texts by the artist explaining his techniques; Günter Meisner.

Leisberg, Alexander. "Neue Tendenzen", *Kunstwerk*, Baden-Baden, vol. 14, nos. 10–11, April-May, 1961, pp. 3–34.

McRoberts and Tunnard Gallery, London, October, 1962, *Piene: Light and Smoke*. Text by the artist.

Galerie Müller, Stuttgart, March 23–April 19, 1963, *Otto Piene*. Text by the artist.

Galerie Alfred Schmela, Dusseldorf, September–October, 1963. *Piene*. Text by the artist.

Galleria Cadario, Milan, June 14–30, 1963, *Piene*. Text by Gillo Dorfles.

MARCEL POUGET

1923, Oran, Algeria. School of Fine Arts, Oran, 1941–42. One-man exhibitions Galerie aux Impressions d'Art, Paris, 1948; Galerie Ariel and Galerie Breteau, Paris, 1962; Galerie Nova Spectra, The Hague, 1963. Resident Paris.

Galerie Ariel and Galerie Breteau, Paris, June 1962, *Pouget*.

R[agon], M[ichel]. "Pouget", *Cimaise*, Paris, vol. 9, no. 60, July–August, 1962, pp. 87, 96.

Ragon, Michel. *Naissance d'un art nouveau*, Paris, Albin Michel, 1963.

Galerie Nova Spectra, The Hague, May 4–June 2, 1963, *M. Pouget*. Text by C. Doelman.

ARNULF RAINER

1929, Vienna. Vienna Kunstakademie. Study trip abroad, 1952–53. One-man exhibition Galerie St. Stephan, Vienna, 1955. Resident Vienna.

Kunstverein für die Rheinlande-Westfalen, Dusseldorf, May 17–June 16, 1957, *Wiener Secession*. Text by A. P. Gütersloh and others.

Neue Galerie der Stadt Linz, July 3–September 6, 1959, *Form und Farbe 1959: Neue Malerie und Plastik in Österreich*. Text by Jorge Lampe.

Galerie St. Stephan, Vienna, and Galerie 55, Aschaffenburg, 1960, *Neue Österreichische Kunst*. Text by Otto Mauer.

JUDIT REIGL

1923, Kapuvar, Hungary. Budapest Academy of Art, 1941–46; two-year fellowship for study in Italy, 1947–48. One-man exhibition Galerie l'Étoile Scellée, Paris, 1954. Resident Paris.

Galerie René Drouin, Paris, October, 1956, *Tensions: Georges, Viseux, Reigl, Hantaï, Degottex*. Text by Hubert Damisch.

Galerie van de Loo, Munich, May–June, 1958, *Judit Reigl*. Text by Clemens Weiler.

Kunstverein Freiburg i.Br., September–October, 1961, *Judit Reigl*. Text by Siegfried Bröse.

"Reigl", *Aujourd'hui*, Boulogne-sur-Seine, vol. 6, no. 36, April, 1962, p. 51.

JEAN-PAUL RIOPELLE

1923, Montreal. To Paris, 1947. One-man exhibition Galerie Nina Dausset, Paris, 1949; Pierre Matisse Gallery, New York, 1963. Resident Paris.

Duthuit, Georges. "Jean-Paul Riopelle", *Numero*, Florence, vol. 4, no. 3, December, 1952, p. 10.

Schneider, Pierre. "Jean-Paul Riopelle", *Yale French Studies*, New Haven, nos. 19–20, 1957, pp. 85–93. [Abridged version in *L'Oeil*, Paris, no. 18, June, 1956, pp. 36–41.]

Wright, Clifford N. "Jean-Paul Riopelle", *Art News and Review*, London, vol. 11, no. 13, July 18, 1959, p. 7.

National Gallery of Canada, Ottawa, 1962, *Jean-Paul Riopelle*. Texts by Charles Comfort, Franco Russoli, Guy Viau, J. Russell Harper, Pierre Schneider.

O'Hara, Frank. "Riopelle: International Speedscapes", *Art News*, New York, vol. 62, no. 2, April, 1963, pp. 32–34, 64–65.

ANTONIO SAURA

1930, Huesca, Spain. First one-man exhibition, Galleria Buchholz, Madrid, 1951. 1953–55, Paris. Founder, *El Paso* group, Madrid, 1957. Exhibits with Pierre Matisse Gallery, New York. Resident Paris.

Saura, Antonio. *Programio*, 1950–51. [Issued as part of *Saura* by Erik Boman, see below.]

Boman, Erik. *Saura*, Madrid, Palacio de Bibliotecas y Museos de Madrid, 1956. [Text in French]

El Paso, Madrid, March, 1958, *Quatro Pintores Espanoles*. Statements by the artist, pp. 7–9.

Conde, Manuel. "La Peinture d'Antonio Saura", *Aujourd'hui*, Boulogne-sur-Seine, vol. 4, no. 23, September, 1959, pp. 22–23.

Cirlot, Juan-Eduardo. "Saura blanc et noir", *Art Actuel International*, Lausanne, vol. 3, no. 15, 1960, pp. 4–5.

Galleria Odyssia, Rome, 1960, *Antonio Saura*. Text by Michel Tapié; "Tres Notas" by the artist.

L'Attico, Rome, October, 1960, *El Paso*. Text by Jean-Eduardo Cirlot; includes manifesto of the group, essay on Saura.

DAVID ALFARO SIQUEIROS

1898, Chihuahua, Mexico. 1919–22, traveled and studied in Belgium, France, Italy, Spain. Imprisoned for political activity, Mexico City, 1962.

Siqueiros, David Alfaro. *No hay mas ruta que la nuestra*, Mexico, 1945.

Siqueiros, D. A. *El Muralismo de Mexico*, Mexico, Ediciones Mexicanas, 1950.

Siqueiros, D. A. *Como se pinta un mural*, Mexico, Ediciones Mexicanas, 1951.

Siqueiros, D. A. *Siqueiros: por la via de una pintura meorrealista o realista social moderna en Mexico*, Mexico, Instituto Nacional de Bellas Artes, 1951. [Text in Spanish, French, English]

Cardoza y Aragon, Luis. "Nuevas notas sobre Alfaro Siqueiros", *Mexico en el arte*, Mexico City, no. 4, October, 1948, pp. 32–48. [Followed by "La Critica del arte como pretexto literario" by Siqueiros, pp. 50–70.]

Valcarcel, Gustavo. "La ultima exposicion de Siqueiros: 5 puntos de objectividad", *Espacios*, Mexico City, no. 32, August, 1956, pp. 58–63. [Concerning the Siqueiros exhibition at the Venice Biennale.]

Myers, Bernard S. *Mexican Painting in Our Time*, New York, Oxford University Press, 1956. [Chapters on Siqueiros: pp. 51–55, 115–119, 167–174, 211–234; bibliography.]

Rodman, Selden. *Mexican Journal*, New York, Devin-Adair, 1958. [Several interviews with Siqueiros interspersed in text.]

K. R. H. SONDERBORG (K. R. H. Hofman)

1923, Sonderborg (Alsen), Denmark. Landeskunstschule, Hamburg, 1947–49; with S. W. Hayter, Paris, 1953. Resident Paris.

G[rohmann], W[ill]. "K.R.H. Sonderborg", *Quadrum*, Brussels, no. 1, 1956, pp. 186–187.

Schmalenbach, Werner. "K.R.H. Sonderborg", *Junge Künstler 58/59: 5 Monographien*, Cologne, Dumont Schauberg, 1959, pp. 41–58.

Ragon, Michel. "Sonderborg", *Cimaise*, Paris, vol. 4, no. 4, March–April, 1959, pp. 24–27.

Grohmann, Will. "K.R.H. Sonderborg", *Quadrum*, Brussels, no. 10, 1961, pp. 131–140.

Flemming, Hans Theodor. "Zehn Jahre Sonderborg", *Kunstwerk*, Baden-Baden, vol. 15, nos. 1–2, July–August, 1961, pp. 27–36.

Galerie Karl Flinker, Paris, October 30–November 30, 1962, *Sonderborg*. Text by Annette Michelson.

YECHESKIEL STREICHMAN

1906, Lithuania. Bezalel School of Art, Jerusalem; Royal Academy of Fine Arts, Florence. Resident Tel Aviv.

Gamzu, Haim. *Painting and Sculpture in Israel*, Tel Aviv, Dvir, 1958, pp. 56–57.

Baram, Sioma. L'Art contemporain en Israel", *L'Art International Contemporain*, [*Prisme des Arts*], Paris, Éditions d'Art et d'Industrie, 1958, p. 178.

Fisher, Yona. "Les Arts Plastiques en Israël", *Aujourd'hui*, Boulogne-sur-Seine, no. 26, April, 1960, pp. 11–26.

PETER STROUD

1921, London. London University Training College, 1947–51; and various art schools. One-man exhibition, ICA, London, 1960. Lecturer in charge of Liberal Studies, Maidstone College of Art, 1961–63. Instructor, Bennington College, Vermont, 1963. Resident U. S.

Stroud, Peter. "The Tensile Image", *Gazette*, London, no. 1, 1961. [on John Plumb, unpaginated].

Stroud, Peter. "The Space Between", *Gazette*, London, no. 2, 1961. [unpaginated].

[Statement on exhibiting in a "Public Situation"] in Crosby, Theo. "UIA Congress Buildings South Bank, London", *Architectural Design*, London, vol. 3, November, 1961, p. 496.

ICA Gallery, London, February 23–April 8, 1960, *Peter Stroud Paintings and Peter Clough Sculpture*. Text on Stroud by Lawrence Alloway.

TERRENCE SYVERSON

1939, Kincaid, Saskatchewan, Canada. University of Saskatchewan Artists' Workshop under Barnett Newman, 1959. Resident New York.

FERNANDO DE SZYSZLO

1925, Lima. School of Fine Arts, Catholic University, Lima, 1944–46. First one-man exhibition, 1947, Peruvian-American Cultural Institute, Lima. Lived in Europe, New York. Visiting critic, Art Department, College of Architecture, Cornell University, 1962. Professor of Art, Catholic University, Lima. Most recent one-man show, White Art Museum, Cornell University, 1963. Resident Lima.

Messer, Thomas M. "Pan America: Contemporary Idioms", *Art in America*, New York, no. 3, 1961, pp. 89, 91–92.

Galería Bonino, Buenos Aires, May, 1961, *De Szyszlo*. Text by José Gomez Sicre.

Institute of Contemporary Art, Boston, Exhibition circulating 1961–62, *Latin America: New Departures*. Statement by the artist.

RUFINO TAMAYO

1899, Oaxaca, Mexico. 1917, Academy, Mexico City. 1933 murals for Mexico City Conservatory. To New York City, 1938. Murals for Smith College, Northampton, Massachusetts, 1943. Exhibits regularly at Knoedler Gallery, New York. Resident Paris.

Tamayo, Rufino [Statement]. *Tiger's Eye*, Westport, Connecticut, no. 1, October, 1947, pp. 61, 63–66.

Jouffroy, Alain. "Portrait d'un artiste: Rufino Tamayo", *Arts*, Paris, no. 655, January 29–February 4, 1958, p. 17. [Interview]

Galerie Beaux-Arts, Paris, November 8–December 9, 1950, *Tamayo*. Texts by Jean Cassou and André Breton.

Knoedler Galleries, New York, November 17–December 12, 1959, *Tamayo*. Text by Jean Cassou.

Paz, Octavio. "Tamayo et la peinture Mexicain", *Cahiers du Musée de Poche*, Paris, no. 1, March, 1959, pp. 80–93.

Cassou, Jean. "Tamayo—Prométhée apportant le feu aux hommes", *Quadrum*, Brussels, no. 6, 1959, pp. 23–25.

ATSUKO TANAKA

1932, Osaka. Academy of Fine Arts, Kyoto and studied with Jiro Yoshihara. Member Gutai group. Resident Osaka.

Ukita, Yozo. "Experimental Outdoor Exhibition of Modern Art to Challenge the Burning Midsummer Sun", *Gutai*, Nishinomiya City, no. 3, October, 1955, p. 24.
Yoshihara, Jiro. "On the Second Outdoor Exhibition of the 'Gutai' Art Group", *Gutai*, Nishinomiya City, no. 5, October, 1956, p. 1.
"The International Art of a New Era", *Gutai*, Nishinomiya City, no. 9, 1958, p. 63. [Special issue as catalogue for Osaka Festival]
Yoshihara, Jiro. "Japan", *Art Forum*, San Francisco, vol. 2, no. 3, 1963, p. 55.

ANTONI TÀPIES

1923, Barcelona. Founding member, group and review *Dau al Set*, 1948. First one-man exhibition, 1950, Galerias Layetanas, Barcelona. Recent one-man exhibition circulating to Museo de Bellas Artes, Caracas; Phoenix Art Center, Pasadena Art Museum; Felix Landau Gallery, Los Angeles, 1962–63. Resident Barcelona.

The Solomon R. Guggenheim Museum, New York, March–April, 1962, *Antoni Tàpies*. Text by Lawrence Alloway. [bibliography]

WILLIAM TURNBULL

1922, Dundee. Slade School of Fine Art, London, 1947–48. Paris, 1948–50. First one-man exhibition, Hanover Gallery, 1950. Latest one-man exhibition. Marlborough-Gerson Galleries, New York, 1963. Since 1951 has taught at Central School of Arts and Crafts, London. Resident, United Kingdom.

The following references refer primarily to Turnbull's painting, not to his sculpture.

"William Turnbull Painter Sculptor", *Uppercase*, London, no. 4, 1960. [Articles and statements by the artist]
Turnbull, William. "The Joining Edge", *Gazette*, London, no. 1, 1961, p. 4.
Turnbull, William. "Images without Temples", *Living Arts*, London, no. 1, 1963, pp. 14–27.
Molton Gallery, London, August 10–September 3, 1960, *William Turnbull: Paintings*. Text by Lawrence Alloway.
Alloway, Lawrence. "The Sculpture and Painting of William Turnbull", *Art International*, Zürich, vol. 5, no. 1, February 1, 1961, pp. 46–52.

VICTOR DE VASARELY

1908, Pecs, Hungary. Studied, Bauhaus, Budapest. 1930, first one-man exhibition, Kovacs Akos Gallery, Budapest. To Paris, 1930. One-man exhibitions, Galerie Denise René, since 1944. Most recent one-man show, Musée des Arts Décoratifs, Paris, 1963. Resident Paris.

Vasarely, Victor de. "Statement", *Art International*, Zürich, vol. 3, no. 8, 1959, pp. 57–59.
Galerie Denise René, Paris, November–December, 1955, *Vasarely*. Text "De l'invention à la re-création" by Vasarely.

Habasque, Guy. "Art et technique: la cinétique", *XXe Siècle*, Paris, vol. 23, no. 17, December, 1961, p. 86, 90, 91, 92.
Musée des Arts Décoratifs, Paris, March–April, 1963, *Vasarely*. Text by Michel Faré. [bibliography]

JORGE DE LA VEGA

1930, Buenos Aires. Exhibitions since 1946. With Galería Bonino, Buenos Aires.

Museo Nacional de Bellas Artes, Buenos Aires, June 15–July 7, 1963, *Deira, Macció, Noé, de la Vega*. Text by Jorge Romero Brest.

BRAM VAN VELDE

1895, Zoeterwoude, near Leyden, The Netherlands. 1922, studied in Germany. To Paris, 1925; from 1926 exhibited regularly at Salon des Indépendants, Surindépendants. First one-man show, 1946, Galerie Mai, Paris. Latest one-man exhibitions Galleria l'Obelisco, Rome, 1962; Galerie Krugier, Geneva, 1962; Knoedler and Co., New York. Resident Paris.

Beckett, Samuel and Duthuit, Georges. "Three Dialogues", *Transition 49*, Paris, no. 5, 1949. On Bram van Velde, pp. 100–103; "Some Sayings of Bram van Velde", p. 104.
Beckett, Samuel, Duthuit, Georges and Putnam, Jacques. *Bram van Velde*, New York, Grove Press, 1958.
Kunsthalle, Berne, May 10–June 15, 1958, *Bram van Velde*. Text by Franz Meyer.
M. Knoedler and Co., New York, February 13–March 10, 1962, *Bram van Velde*. [bibliography]

JIRO YOSHIHARA

1904, Osaka. One-man exhibition Asahi Kaisan, Osaka, 1928. Member *Nika-Kai* Society; founded Gutai Art Association, 1953. Resident Ashiya City, Hyogo.

Yoshihara, Jiro. "On the First Gutai-Ten", *Gutai*, Nishinomiya City, no. 4, July, 1956, p. 2.
Yoshihara, Jiro. "On the Second Outdoor Exhibition of the 'Gutai' Art Group", *Gutai*, Nishinomiya City, no. 5, October, 1956, p. 1.
Yoshihara, Jiro. "Gutai Art on the Stage", *Gutai*, Nishinomiya City, no. 7, July, 1957, insert.
Yoshihara, Jiro. "The International Art of a New Era", *Gutai*, Nishinomiya City, no. 9, 1958, p. 7. [Special issue as catalogue for Osaka Festival.]
Ashton, Dore. "Japanese Avantgardism", *Arts and Architecture*, Los Angeles, vol. 75, no. 11, November, 1958, p. 4–5, 34.
Tapié, Michel and Haga, Tôre. *Avante-garde Art in Japan*, New York, Abrams, 1962.

RICARDO YRARRÁZAVAL

1931, Santiago, Chile. School of Fine Arts, Rome, 1952; Académie Julian, Paris, 1953. One-man exhibition, Santiago, 1954. Resident Santiago.

Romera, Antonio. *Historia de la Pintura Chilena*, Santiago, Zig-zag, 1960, p. 155.

JURY GUGGENHEIM INTERNATIONAL AWARD 1964

DR. WERNER HAFTMANN   HANS HOFMANN   DR. ARNOLD RÜDLINGER

*Since its inception, the Guggenheim International Award of
$10,000 has been conferred upon the following painters: Ben
Nicholson in 1956; Joan Miró in 1958; Karel Appel in 1960.
In addition, 19 National Section Awards and 3 Continental
Section Awards of $1,000 each were made in 1956. In 1958,
22 artists received National Section Awards, and 1 Extra
National Award of $1,000 was made. 27 National Section
Awards, and 1 Extra National Award of $1,000 were made in
1960.*

*As in previous years, the Guggenheim International Award is
a grant of $10,000. In addition, five awards of $2,500 each
will be conferred by the jury.*

THE SOLOMON R. GUGGENHEIM MUSEUM

STAFF

Director	*Thomas M. Messer*
Curator	*Lawrence Alloway*
Associate Curator	*Louise Averill Svendsen*
Assistant Curator	*Daniel Robbins*
Research Fellows	*Carol Fuerstein and Maurice Tuchman*
Librarian	*Mary Joan Hall*
Membership	*Carol Tormey*
Registrar	*Arlene B. Dellis*
Conservation	*Orrin Riley and Saul Fuerstein*
Photography	*Robert E. Mates*
Custodian	*Jean Xceron*
Business Administrator	*Glenn H. Easton, Jr.*
Administrative Assistant	*Viola H. Gleason*
Office Manager	*Agnes R. Connolly*
Building Superintendent	*Peter G. Loggin*
Head Guard	*George J. Sauve*

Exhibition 64/1   *January, February, March 1964*

5000 copies of this catalogue, designed by Herbert Matter
have been produced by Fred M. Kleeberg Associates
in December 1963
for the Trustees of The Solomon R. Guggenheim Foundation
on the occasion of the exhibition
Guggenheim International Award 1964